YOUR PERSONALITY AND YOU
WORKBOOK

YOUR PERSONALITY YOU

AND

WORKBOOK

YAEL DENNIS, PhD, MD

Exercises
to Better
Understand
Yourself
and Who
You Want
to Be

ROCKRIDGE PRESS

First Rockridge Press trade paperback edition 2022

Rockridge Press and the Rockridge Press logo are trademarks or registered trademarks of Callisto Media Inc. and/or its affiliates in the United States and other countries and may not be used without written permission.

For general information on our other products and services, please contact our Customer Care Department within the United States at (866) 744-2665, or outside the United States at (510) 253-0500.

Paperback ISBN: 978-1-63878-583-5 | ebook ISBN: 978-1-63878-693-1

Manufactured in the United States of America

Interior and Cover Designer: John Calmeyer
Art Producer: Melissa Malinowsky
Editor: Brian Sweeting
Production Editor: Jax Berman
Production Manager: Lanore Coloprisco

Illustrations © LEROY Design/Creative Market; Author photo courtesy of Matt Dubin, PhD

10 9 8 7 6 5 4 3 2 1 0

*To Matt, my companion in growth
and my reward for doing the work.*

CONTENTS

INTRODUCTION

Prepare to amaze yourself. You're about to set off on a journey that will bring out the best in you. You may not have thought that making deep personal changes could be an enjoyable and rewarding experience, but by the end of this book you'll find yourself happier and more fulfilled, with better relationships and a more positive sense of your future.

I have devoted decades to studying what makes people tick and how to motivate them to change for the better. My fascination with human behavior began when I was a child. I grew up in a tough area of town, in a home connected to a tavern. My world was filled with wonderful people living difficult lives. What was it, I wondered, that led them to cycles of addiction, violence, poverty, and despair? And what would it take for them to believe in themselves and live differently?

My passion for understanding human suffering and personal growth led me to a fifteen-year career as a child and adolescent psychiatrist. I learned numerous theories about how personality is formed and how adults can learn and grow, even if they experienced traumatic childhoods or suffered from biologically based mental illnesses.

After retiring from that career, I taught at the college level and served as the chair of the Department of Health Sciences and Sustainability at a community college. Along the way, I earned a master's degree in sustainability and a doctorate in religious studies. I also took advantage of every opportunity for leadership training that was available. I learned even more about why people do what they do and how they can learn to do different things, not from the perspective of mental illness, but through the lenses of sociology, learning theories, and positive psychology.

Not surprisingly, I applied these theories to myself. My own journey required me to learn, grow, and change. Not only have I used the lessons and exercises in this book with clients and students, but I have also tested them in my own life. They have worked for others, they have worked for me, and they will work for you.

Above all, what I hope you get out of this book is a sense of your own amazing potential and an idea of how you can grow into your best self. Sometimes personal growth can be scary; changes may happen so quickly that you're not sure what awaits. Other times, change might happen so slowly that you feel you're not getting anywhere. Feeling stuck in one place can lead you to feelings of frustration or disappointment, and you may want to give up. But if you keep working at becoming the best possible version of yourself, you'll indeed be amazed. You'll look back on those times when you felt stuck, and you'll see that a whole lot of change was happening under the surface.

Your own curiosity will be your best support in this journey. You'll start with an exploration of your highest values and best strengths. Your values will be your guidepost, and your strengths will be your walking stick. Along the way, you'll have opportunities to reflect on your past experiences, choices, and behaviors. The purpose of these exercises is for you to learn more deeply about your own innermost needs, not to cause you to berate yourself or feel guilty. Instead of relying on old unquestioned assumptions and unexamined habits that you may have led with in the past, you'll develop a plan to use your strengths and lead from your best qualities.

The privilege of a lifetime is being who you are.

—JOSEPH CAMPBELL

HOW TO USE THIS BOOK

When read from beginning to end, this book will equip you with the knowledge, skills, and habits of mind needed to become the very best possible version of yourself. Knowledge is the starting point. First, you'll learn about the leading theories in the field of psychology. Chapters 1 and 2 review personality theories and what psychologists have learned so far about how people grow and change. Then you'll begin to deepen your self-knowledge. Chapter 3 asks you to take stock of who you are and where you've been. By the end of these chapters, you'll have a clear sense of your values, strengths, visions, and goals. These are the navigational tools you'll use throughout the rest of the book.

Chapters 4 through 8 will deepen both your self-knowledge and your knowledge of the change process, while also showing you how to develop the skills and habits of mind that will help you reach your personal goals. These chapters lead you through the journey of change one step at a time, giving you just-in-time knowledge that will further your growth, as well as applied exercises to deepen your learning.

Chapter 4 will help you set goals you're passionate enough about to give you the energy and commitment you need to reach them. You'll learn how to take concrete action while maintaining a growth mindset in chapter 5. Chapter 6 will show you the benefits of keeping track of your progress, and you'll learn the importance of celebrating small achievements on your way to the larger goals. Turning obstacles into stepping-stones to success is the main focus of chapter 7, because let's face it: If you weren't facing obstacles to change, you would have changed already. Setbacks and challenges are part of every change process. In fact, if you're willing to learn from them, you can use each of them to your advantage. Finally, in chapter 8, you'll learn the most powerful habit of mind for keeping yourself inspired on your growth journey: self-love. You'll also discover how self-love leads to better relationships and deeper connections with others in your life (and *not* to selfishness, as you may have been taught).

This book is *your* book, and it's *your* change journey. If one chapter or exercise speaks to you, feel free to skip to that part and dive in.

If you want to take your work even deeper, the companion journal *Your Personality and You Journal: Prompts and Practices to Better Understand Yourself, Reflect, and Grow* offers more prompts and practices to help you deepen your experience. Both that book and this one are great stand-alone guides, and together they will give you an even richer and more well-rounded approach to growth.

This book will be therapeutic in that you'll experience a greater quality of life when you feel empowered to become the best version of yourself, but it's not a substitute for psychotherapy or other mental health treatments. If you're struggling with depression, anxiety, post-traumatic stress disorder, hallucinations, or other psychological conditions that make it difficult or impossible for you to function (for example, getting out of bed, showering, or getting to work), please seek the assistance of a psychotherapist or psychiatrist who can provide you with appropriate mental health care.

The Self is in everybody. . . . And the Self possesses its own wisdom about how to heal internal and external relationships.

—RICHARD C. SCHWARTZ

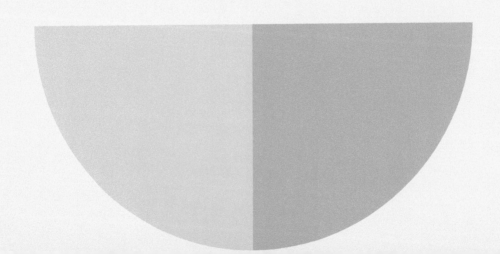

CHAPTER 1

Let's Talk about Personality

Does "personality" refer to a person's character traits, such as reliability or kindness? Or does it refer to a person's emotional traits, such as calmness or irritability, that might also be viewed as temperament? Is personality the result of someone's genetics or upbringing? If you're uncertain, you're not alone; even experts in the field of psychology frequently disagree about how to answer these important questions. As it turns out, there are many theories about what personality is and how it functions, and which parts of it can be changed.

This chapter will provide a basic overview of personality theories and an explanation of some common personality tests and how to use them to your advantage. We'll conclude with the idea of personality as a story you tell yourself.

The exercises in this book draw from the best of several personality theories to maximize the benefit to you, and this foundational information will help you learn about how each of these exercises contributes to the personality changes you're working toward.

A Brief History of Personality

Do you often wonder what makes people tick? Why some people have cheerful personalities and others have hostile ones? Is personality hereditary or learned? If you've asked yourself these questions, you're not alone. Throughout the ages, great thinkers have devoted time and attention to trying to decipher the mysteries of human personality. And much like personalities themselves, the leading theories on personality have changed quite a bit over time.

Thousands of years ago, personality was assumed to be connected to the physical body, if not determined by it. For example, in Indian traditional medicine, known as Ayurveda, personality is viewed as having both physical and psychological components. The Ayurvedic *tridosha* system, developed in ancient India, shows how personality types and physical health correlate. Almost every system of traditional medicine has a similar theory.

Western medicine drew heavily from Greek philosophy. Ancient Greeks believed that personality was related to one of four different "humors," or bodily fluids, and it varied based on which was most prevalent in a person's body. The humors were blood, phlegm, black bile, and yellow bile, and the corresponding personality traits were described as sanguine (happy), phlegmatic (bland), melancholic (depressed), and choleric (hostile). This understanding of the intertwining of personality with the body was the primary worldview among Europeans for many centuries.

These terms may seem odd, given that they're based on a worldview that we no longer share, but they can still be useful. In fact, although these terms originated in ancient Greece, they were used recently enough that fans of the works of Charles Dickens or Jane Austen may recognize them. They can be useful because the term "personality" is vague and ever changing, much like the phenomenon it describes.

Now, it's easy to see why someone whose body is filled with black bile would be at least a little depressed and in poor health. But most personality traits don't relate to physical traits or bodily health in any direct way. We've all heard of people who had cancer and kept a great attitude, and you likely know at least one person who is in great physical health but is still cranky most of the time. What's more, personality doesn't relate directly to one's environment, either.

Many people experiencing poverty are kind and outgoing with a great sense of humor. Others seem to have it all, yet struggle with depression or anxiety despite the apparent luxuries in their lives.

Additionally, personality traits sometimes don't relate to one another over time all that well. If you search your memory, you probably remember someone you knew in school who has changed significantly since then. Or perhaps you know someone who has experienced a huge change in their circumstances that led to their personality changing as well. This is actually great news because it means that people can change. *You* can change, and you can be the director of these changes if you choose to.

Modern Theories of Personality

Theories of personality changed dramatically in the wake of Sigmund Freud's groundbreaking work in the early twentieth century. Freud hypothesized that the mind, or psyche, is composed of at least three major parts: the *ego*, the *superego*, and the *id*. The ego is the part that people are aware (or conscious) of, and it's responsible for helping us meet our needs in ways that maintain our reputation. According to Freud, the id is largely outside of our awareness, and it's where most of our sexual and aggressive drives are housed. Although we're unaware of it, the id is often the driver of our actions. The superego is largely unconscious, and it's a bit like an inner police force that is responsible for restraining our impulses.

Many other theorists emerged in the wake of Freud, some of whom elaborated on his original ideas in innovative ways while also rejecting one or another of his key concepts. These theorists include Carl Jung, Heinz Kohut, and Karen Horney, who promote what are called "psychodynamic theories" of personality that are based on Freud's theories and are heavily concerned with the unconscious mind. Psychodynamic theories hold that an adult's personality is largely the product of their childhood experiences. Although psychodynamic theories suggest that childhood experiences account for personality, they were not developed through the study of children; instead, these theories were based on adult patients' recollections of their childhoods.

Other theories are rooted in entirely different worldviews. Swiss psychologist Jean Piaget was among the first theorists to study children, observing them over time to see how they learn. Various learning theories such as cognitive psychology, behaviorism, and social learning theory were developed in his footsteps, each promoting the idea that human personality is the result of learning, rather than genetics, and that personality is shaped by the environment in which people live. Humanist thinkers such as Carl Rogers and Abraham Maslow also brought their philosophy to the world of psychology.

Still other theorists, referred to as "trait theorists," focus on personality traits. Raymond Cattell developed a sixteen-factor model based on different personality traits. More recently, the Big Five model posits five crucial traits: agreeableness, conscientiousness, extraversion, neuroticism, and openness to experience. As you might expect, the precise number of traits required to adequately describe personality is hotly debated.

Proponents of each school of thought view their theory as ideal. However, psychologist Stewart E. Cooper demonstrated that experienced counselors who adhered to different theories tended to perform the same interventions as one another, regardless of their different understandings of personality. Each of the theories contributes something vital to our understanding of human personality and how it develops over time. They can explain things we have observed about ourselves, and they show us new aspects of personality that we had never noticed before. Above all, they give us new tools for learning about ourselves and others around us and a new language for describing what we see.

Personality Is a Story You Tell Yourself (and Everyone Else)

One of the newer theories of personality that you'll read about time and again in this book is the Internal Family Systems (or IFS) model, developed by Dr. Richard Schwartz. In this theory, much like in Freud's theory, the personality is viewed as being composed of multiple parts, but the similarity ends there.

According to the IFS model, a person has a core *Self* that can be described with eight traits: calmness, clarity, compassion, confidence, connection, courage, creativity, and curiosity. These are known in the IFS model as "the 8 Cs of Self." You have access to these traits in the core of your Self, even if you don't experience them all the time. Every person has a core Self that exhibits calmness, clarity, and so on, and every person also has personality parts that have developed to keep them safe from harm.

Exiles are very vulnerable parts that keep pain from past harm locked away from our awareness as much as possible. They typically develop in response to various types of traumas. There are "small-t traumas," such as being left with a kind aunt while your mom was in the hospital when you were three years old. Your life was not at risk, but you may have felt terrified and sad at the time, and these emotions may have been buried deep inside you.

Other parts, known as *protectors*, come in two varieties. They navigate our lives to minimize risk of harm. They may respond to a small-t trauma by making sure you're never left alone again, or they could ensure that you never get so attached to someone that you become anxious when they leave.

Some parts are also formed in response to "large-T Traumas": instances in which there was real risk of bodily harm, such as witnessing domestic violence, experiencing physical or sexual abuse, or even being involved in a serious traffic accident. Parts that develop in response to extreme events will be extreme themselves. If you're struggling with extreme parts, please see the Resources section in the back of this book for information on how to find a qualified therapist.

When seen through the lens of the IFS model, a personality could be viewed as a story you tell yourself. Self, protectors, and exiles can be viewed as characters in that story. Sometimes the parts may have been writing your story without much input from the Self. When the parts take over, this is referred to as "blending" or "hijacking" in the IFS model. In this workbook, you'll learn how to use the IFS model and other personality theories as tools to help you access your inner resources (and acquire new ones) so that you can become the author of your own story. With patience and persistence, you can write a new story line in which your parts come into a different, joyful, and more productive relationship with one another. As you write this new story, different traits and characteristics will come to the forefront. That is what growth and development are all about.

WHAT PERSONALITY IS NOT

Even though "personality" is a vague term that itself refers to a vague phenomenon, it doesn't include everything about a person, such as one's taste in clothing, physical appearance, likes and dislikes, and so on. These preferences contribute to or express aspects of one's personality, but they are not the types of traits that are generally included in the understanding of personality.

For example, one person with multiple tattoos may be deeply compassionate, but another person with multiple tattoos might be aggressive. The outer appearance does not reveal the inner core. If two specific people are both Red Sox fans, that does not mean they will become close friends.

These superficial factors don't indicate whether a person has integrity, whether they can navigate conflict with kindness, whether they crave solitude, or whether they are prone to viewing life pessimistically. As you'll learn throughout this book, there's much more to personality, and when you put your mind to it, your personality can change much more rapidly than your taste in clothing.

That said, a personality is typically relatively consistent. Even so, overwhelming stress can bring out the worst in anyone. Job loss, divorce, or a serious illness might result in temporary irritability or emotional sensitivity. The exercises in this book can help you build resilience, but don't judge yourself negatively if you're going through a hard time.

We'll discuss change theory later in this book, but for now, it's important simply to know that change is possible. Many character traits can be learned with practice. If you're prone to being short-tempered, you can develop more calmness in the face of stress. You may never become as calm as your Uncle Fred, but you can certainly become much calmer than you are now.

Personality Tests and What They Mean

If you have a social media account, you've likely encountered some form of personality test. Often these tests are whimsical, indicating which character you would be in the *Harry Potter* movies or in a television series. In other cases, the tests are the result of rigorous scientific study. Either way, you may or may not like the results, and you may come away feeling as if the test missed one or another of your key personality traits.

What all these tests have in common is that they're tools that serve different purposes. Sometimes they function as entertainment; other times, they're useful as diagnostic tools; and in still other cases, they're simply a way to deepen your self-understanding.

Big Five Inventory (BFI): The Big Five Inventory corresponds to the Big Five model and measures the dimensions described in that model: extraversion vs. introversion, agreeableness vs. antagonism, conscientiousness vs. lack of direction, neuroticism vs. emotional stability, and openness vs. closedness to experience.

Minnesota Multiphasic Personality Inventory (MMPI): This inventory has been rigorously demonstrated to be a reliable indicator of psychopathology. It is most commonly administered by clinicians for diagnostic purposes.

Myers-Briggs Type Indicator (MBTI): This test is grounded in the psychological approach of Carl Jung and results in an assignment to one of sixteen personality types. Each type has its own four-letter code indicating the combination of your *preferences* in four different domains: extraversion or introversion (E or I), sensing or intuition (S or N), thinking or feeling (T or F), and judging or perceiving (J or P). It's important to note that the MBTI is a measure of preferences, not of pathology, distress, or challenges you might experience based on these preferences.

Positive Psychology: The following two tests have their roots in the field of positive psychology: the study of happy, successful individuals and the character traits that contribute to their well-being. Because of its emphasis on what is desirable in personality, positive psychology is a fantastic navigational tool. It can help you determine desired end goals and the skills and habits of mind that will help you achieve them.

CliftonStrengths Assessment: This assessment was originally developed by the psychologist Don Clifton, whose driving question was "What would happen if we studied what was *right* with people?" The results of this test assign a series of thirty-four natural personality "talents" in ranked order. Over time, a person's top ten talents tend to remain unchanged. However, with increased investment in the form of expanding your knowledge about the talent and your habit of using it, you can turn your natural talent into a strength.

VIA Character Strengths Assessment: This test is offered for free by the VIA Institute on Character and is loosely correlated with the CliftonStrengths Assessment. It is scientifically validated and, like the CliftonStrengths Assessment, emphasizes what you're good at already. Results come in the form of a ranked order of twenty-four character strengths that are present to some degree in each person.

What You Can (and Maybe Can't) Change

The purpose of this book is to help you develop personality traits that you value so that you can be the best possible version of yourself. This is only possible because *change* is possible. It takes effort to acquire the knowledge, skills, and habits of mind that will enable change, but that effort pays off.

Absolutely central to the change process is learning about something called the "growth mindset." This term was developed by psychologist Carol Dweck (2008) in her groundbreaking work about the power of mindset in all manner of successful endeavors: business, parenting, school, and even relationships. In contrast to the growth mindset is something Dweck identified as the "fixed mindset."

Those who have a fixed mindset believe that all abilities and traits, such as intelligence, athleticism, economic success, and so on, are determined at birth. Because people with a fixed mindset don't believe they can change, they tend to hide their mistakes rather than learn from them, and this dismissal of their own ability to change tends to be a self-fulfilling prophecy.

People with a growth mindset, on the other hand, believe that growth and change are possible. Because they don't believe that they're limited by their current abilities, they tend to improve themselves over time. They are more inclined to learn from their mistakes than to hide them. Because they focus on continued growth rather than innate ability, they end up succeeding more than those with a fixed mindset. They're more excited than intimidated by challenging obstacles.

The good news is that Dweck's research reveals that a growth mindset can be learned. If you saw yourself in the description of someone with a fixed mindset, don't worry. Mindset is not fixed, and a growth mindset can be learned.

I'll provide an example from my own personal experience. According to my CliftonStrengths Assessment, "adaptability" is ranked number thirty-one of the thirty-four talents on my list. In the past, I didn't handle last-minute changes to schedules, deadlines, or plans very well at all. In fact, I used to become anxious or annoyed by them. But since I learned that adaptability is not high on my list, when those feelings arise, I recognize them as just my low adaptability rearing its ugly head. I then use self-management techniques to help myself stay calm, cool, and collected. I still prefer when things go according to plan, of course, but my day is no longer ruined when they don't.

Because so many personality traits can be learned and practiced, it's hard to say where the limits of your growth might be. Based on the tenets of positive psychology, you'd do best by making the most of your strengths and using them to overcome your weaknesses. According to change theory, it takes at least six weeks to develop a new habit, and setbacks are normal. Of course, at some point you'll have to accept what you can't change, but right now it's too soon to tell what that will be.

Writing a New Story for Yourself

Once upon a time at a conference I attended, a speaker uttered the words "Hard hearts tell old stories." My life changed that very day. I had been going through a lot of drama in the aftermath of a messy divorce, and I was still holding on to a lot of bitterness and hurt feelings about it all. When I heard the speaker say that hard hearts tell old stories, I realized that I had to stop telling old stories and start writing new ones.

I invite you to start writing your own new story, too. What story could you tell that would inspire you, and everyone who knows you, to dream big? What story could you tell that would give you the energy to get out of the bed in the morning and do what needs to be done to live that story? What will have changed about you and the way you live your life by the end of the story?

If you enjoy meditating or journaling, this might be a great place to allow yourself to daydream about the characters in your story. Think back to the IFS personality model described on pages 4 and 5 and get curious about the cast of characters in your story. Which parts of your personality are in favor of making changes? Which parts are skeptical? Which tender parts need more care? Throughout this book, you'll have opportunities to get to know these parts, to hear their concerns, and to form overall happier relationships with them.

You'll also have opportunities to reflect on the past chapters of your life story. In doing so, you'll learn about the emotional needs and behavioral habits that have been writing your story until now. These needs and habits led you to whatever circumstances now inspire you to change. Because the past led to the present, a fixed mindset might conclude that the present is unchangeable because the past is unchangeable. But this is not at all the case.

In this book, you'll learn how to cultivate and practice a growth mindset. You'll identify the emotional needs that, because they are unmet, drive your behaviors. And you'll create a plan to meet those needs in ways that are more uplifting for you. You'll also identify the habits of mind and behavior that haven't brought about the results you crave, and you'll learn which new habits might work better for you.

Then, throughout the remaining chapters of your own life story, you can reorient to a growth mindset. Like in any good story (take *Star Wars*, for example), you'll encounter challenges. But with each page you turn, you'll come one step closer to the best version of yourself. Given that it's possible to grow throughout your entire life, you'll probably never reach that goal. But because continued growth *is* the goal, you'll always succeed.

How are your thoughts, actions, and feelings affecting your life?

Not at all   Significantly
1   2   3   4   5

How much better would you feel about yourself if you could change your patterns of thinking?

Not much   Significantly
1   2   3   4   5

How much would your life improve if you changed your problem behaviors?

I can't change them   I would be happier and more successful
1   2   3   4   5

How likely do you think it is that you'll be able to change things about yourself that you don't like?

Not very   I will probably succeed, at least partially
1   2   3   4   5

How important is it to make these changes?

Not very   It is my top priority
1   2   3   4   5

······································ **RESULTS** ······································

5 to 14: You might be struggling to find reasons to change.

15 to 20: You're willing to try changing even if you're a bit skeptical.

21 to 25: You're ready to become the best version of yourself.

Key Takeaways

- Throughout the ages, great thinkers have pondered what exactly is meant by the term "personality" and why personalities develop the way they do. Most theorists have focused on what's "wrong" with people. Positive psychology, a relatively recently developed field, focuses on what goes "right."

- If personality can be viewed as a story you tell yourself and others, then every personality theory amounts to a different way of telling the same story. No one way of telling that story maps onto any given person's life perfectly. But you can pick from each of these theories a way to tell your own story that makes continued growth not only possible but likely.

- Some personality tests can help you identify areas for growth or strengths that can help you along the way. Take what's helpful for yourself, and leave the rest. They are tools for your use, not limits to your potential.

- The purpose of this book is to help you grow into the fullest and most satisfied and successful version of yourself possible. However, it's important to recognize that part of growth is accepting both your own and other people's imperfections.

- A growth mindset is key to making lasting change. If you have a fixed mindset, don't worry. You can change that, too. A growth mindset can be learned, and you'll have plenty of opportunities to practice throughout this book.

Now, let's get busy writing a new story of you!

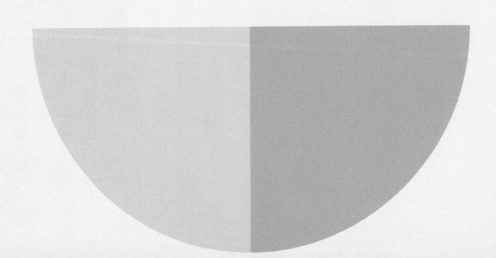

At present you need to live the question. Perhaps you will gradually, without even noticing it, find yourself experiencing the answer, some distant day.

—RAINER MARIA RILKE

CHAPTER 2

How to Nurture Self-Growth

In chapter 1, we reviewed the basics of personality theory. In this chapter, we'll review the basics of personality *change*. In deciding to change and grow on your own, you'll be joining millions of others who have taken the reins of their own lives and decided to become their best selves. Psychologists have taken notice of these remarkable people and have learned quite a bit from them about how to make change happen. You, too, can benefit from the experiences of others by learning how they transformed their lives and what they encountered along the way. There's no way to make it easy, but, armed with this knowledge, you'll more easily navigate the unavoidable challenges you'll face on the road to self-growth.

What Is Self-Growth?

What does "personal growth" even mean? If you have a sense that at the "end" of your growth process you should be perfect, or even just perfectly happy, you'll no doubt be disappointed. No human being is perfect, and emotions shift over time in response to circumstances. Besides which, there's no "end" to personal growth. It's an ongoing process of developing skills that enhance your inner sense of well-being, your ability to form close and satisfying relationships with other people, and your capacity to deal with the changes of life while still getting dinner on the table (more or less).

One way to describe self-growth is through metaphor. You may have heard Jon Kabat-Zinn discussing the aphorism: "You can't stop the waves, but you can learn to surf." What this saying means is that life has a way of bringing changes that challenge us: the "waves." There's no way to stop these challenges from arriving on your doorstep. From this perspective, self-growth might mean something like "learning to surf."

In my own work, I take this metaphor a step further. Growth is not just about learning to surf on the waves; it's also about growing to the extent that you can navigate larger waves. Toy boats capsize easily, rowboats less so, but you'd hardly take a rowboat across the Atlantic. Ocean liners, on the other hand, handle massive waves without capsizing. Personal growth means something along the lines of becoming a seaworthy vessel capable of sailing rough seas without capsizing completely. It gives you the ability to deal with what life sends your way. There's no such thing as an unsinkable ship, however. Personal growth in this metaphor also means that you learn how to steer toward calmer waters and recognize when you need to pick up that radio and call for help.

Others describe personal growth as providing "more room" for their personality. With this growth, you'd still be yourself, but you'd be less reactive to things going on inside or around you. You'd be better able to express yourself and listen to others without hurt feelings or heated conflict being the result.

Personal growth may equip you with a longer fuse so that you don't get as angry as quickly as you used to. You may gain a better sense of the big picture, so you're less likely to become overwhelmed or depressed by setbacks, surprises, disappointments, or losses.

Using the IFS-informed approach described in chapter 1, you'll experience greater *calmness* and *clarity* on a regular basis. You'll be less inclined to take others' struggles and weaknesses personally or to view them judgmentally. Instead, you'll understand that other people have their own needs and limitations that have nothing to do with you. You'll become *curious* about their experiences, and you'll be able to respond *creatively* in the moment. In short, you'll be more *compassionate* with others, as well as with yourself. All of this will lead to a greater sense of *connection* with those you love and more *confidence* within yourself.

Self-Limiting Beliefs

Human beings are storytelling creatures. Fairy tales, legends, myths, parables—these are the stories that humans have learned and grown from throughout the ages. Every culture tells tales of how the world came to be as it is, and every culture reveals its ideals through stories. Similarly, personal growth requires that you tell yourself new stories about who you are, what you value, and how you operate in the world.

As with any great story, your story likely already has many chapters, a general plotline, and a few different subplots. Some conflict or goal has likely arisen in your story, and you've probably faced obstacles along the way to resolving that conflict or reaching the goal. Perhaps the desire for resolution and frustration about these challenges led you to pick up this book.

This moment right here of you with this book in your hand is the plot twist you've been waiting for. The main character turns out to be very different than you'd been led to believe. The world around you is not quite what you thought.

In other words, you likely hold some self-limiting beliefs about yourself or the world around you. Throughout the course of this workbook, you'll learn that things are not precisely what you thought they were.

How did you come to be so mistaken about yourself and the world around you? From the moment we're born, we all receive messages about ourselves from our parents, our teachers, our friends, and the other people in our lives. We receive praise or criticism, experience trauma, or endure shameful events, and we start to believe that those instances define us. If we're a member of a minority group or are physically disabled or are different in some other way, we may receive even more frequent and more negative feedback from other people because of their biases and judgment. These experiences affect our self-image, and they shape how we see the world.

Throughout this book, you'll be asked to shed these limiting beliefs and replace them with inspiring thoughts about your potential for growth and the possibility that the world around you may support or even nurture what is best in you. Changing the story you tell about yourself will require practice, patience, and commitment. You'll have to start by telling a story that is at least somewhat believable. If you don't believe it at least a little bit, you won't be inspired or confident enough to take the steps needed to make the story real. Next, you'll begin to tell uplifting stories about your intentions for the future, which will inspire you to act in alignment with those intentions.

In each chapter, I'll call attention to various self-limiting beliefs that are common to each stage of growth, and I'll suggest a few options for how you can problem-solve and move past those beliefs in believable ways.

Getting Started with Self-Growth

The personal growth process is often described using the metaphor of a journey. Before setting off on any journey, it's a good idea to have a sense of where you'll end up and how you'll get there. The approach we take in this book centers on the metaphor of telling a new story about yourself as a way to highlight the intentional personality changes you'll be working toward. I invite you to combine the two and consider the possibility that the new story you're writing is an epic adventure.

In this story, the main character awakens to discover that the person they deeply desire to be is in fact the person they are meant to be. Even more exciting is the passage where they realize that the power to transform themselves had been inside them all along. In *The Wizard of Oz*, Dorothy learns that she was wearing the key to the way home on her feet the whole time; in *Star Wars*, Luke realizes that the Force is already within him; and in *The Lord of the Rings*, Frodo accepts that he, and only he, is the one to destroy the One Ring. Similarly, you'll come to know that you, too, have the power to rise to life's challenges.

Using tried-and-true storytelling techniques, you'll get a better idea of how to write a new story of you that delights you. The following is a brief preview of what's in store.

TAKING AN HONEST LOOK AT YOURSELF AND YOUR PAST

Typically, the first act of the three-act story structure introduces us to the character by way of a few key scenes that give us an idea of who we're dealing with. As the character develops, we learn more about how their past shaped their present. At the exact time we're learning about their past, they are in the process of developing their heroic characteristics. How did the character get to be this way? What happened in their past that led them to think and act as they do? Where did they acquire their strengths and weaknesses? What is important to them? Who are they, and how do we know who they are? This is known as a character's backstory.

In chapter 3, you'll begin to sketch your own backstory. You'll tell a few key stories that help you see yourself differently. You'll see how you developed the way you did, and you'll start to visualize some of the key self-limiting beliefs that you carry as a result. You'll get a clearer sense of what you value and why. And you'll begin to correct those self-limiting beliefs right from the beginning with exercises that will call attention to the strengths you already have but usually overlook.

SETTING GOALS WITH A PURPOSE

The conflict around which every great story revolves arises when the main character wants something of value they don't yet have. Dorothy wanted to go home. Luke wanted to become a Jedi. Frodo wanted to destroy the One Ring once and for all. Perhaps you've had a life-changing experience that made your goal crystal clear. Maybe that's why you picked up this workbook: You know precisely *what* needs to change, but you just don't know *how* to change it.

Either way, chapter 4 will be essential for your change journey: It will provide you with exercises that will reveal your deepest desires for growth and change.

What do you want to be, do, or have at the end of your new story? What will it take for you to become the best version of yourself? What knowledge must you obtain? What skills must you acquire? What new habits must you develop?

These exercises will build on those from chapter 3. Each of your goals will be aligned with your values and supported by your strengths. That way, you'll have more than enough inspiration and dedication to do the work needed to reach the goal.

TAKING ACTION AND FORMING THE HABITS YOU WANT

Even though the heroes in our well-known stories had the strength within them all along, they still had to take action to discover their heroic nature. Dorothy follows the yellow brick road. Luke travels to Dagobah to study with Jedi Master Yoda. Frodo sets out for Mordor. However, a vision without a plan is a dream, so chapter 5 will provide you with exercises to help you generate an action plan to achieve the changes that are most meaningful for you.

What steps will you take, and what path will you follow? You'll learn about "SMART goals" (see page 59), which will help you break down those larger objectives into manageable chunks so you don't get overwhelmed by all the change required to reach your goal. Action steps will be identified, giving you a clear road map to acquiring the knowledge, skills, and habits of mind you need to reach your larger goal. You'll set timelines for action steps that work for your personal schedule. Finally, you'll create benchmarks and check-in points so you can periodically assess whether things are going according to plan and whether that plan needs to be revised.

TRACKING YOUR GROWTH AND CELEBRATING SUCCESS

Once you've outlined your backstory (that is, you've taken a good look at your past), identified the inspiring goal that motivates you to change (set goals that have meaning for you), and found the road you must take to achieve that goal (created an action plan), you'll begin writing your new story one chapter at a time. In other words, start the process of keeping track of your accomplishments and celebrating each success. One of the major benefits of inserting benchmarks into your action plan is that they give you plenty of opportunity to celebrate your successes. You'll also quickly notice when things aren't going according to plan and be able to troubleshoot.

Taking the time to celebrate your successes will help you stay motivated to keep working on your plan; but to celebrate your successes, you'll need to keep track of your progress. Chapter 6 offers exercises that will help you monitor your progress, celebrate your achievements, and note when your plan may need a few adjustments. You can use a calendar, smartphone, spreadsheet, or another tool to create a plan for inspiring and recording your progress along the way.

TACKLING OBSTACLES AND EMBRACING FAILURE

No epic adventure would be complete without a few obstacles. If Dorothy had immediately realized that she had the power to return home, it wouldn't have made for much of a story. At the end of *The Empire Strikes Back*, it seems as if all hope has been lost. Frodo's encounters with Shelob and Gollum (not to mention the Ring itself) keep us on the edge of our seats. Heroes overcome these failures and setbacks by reaching out for help, reaching in for strength, or simply trying again (and again) until they get it right.

You, too, will encounter obstacles and setbacks as you write your new story of you. Transforming obstacles into stepping-stones and failures into fuel will be crucial to reaching your ultimate goal of becoming the best possible version of yourself. Setbacks and failures are part of your epic adventure, just like the fictional ones that keep us so entertained. Exercises to help you reach out for help, find your own inner strength, or simply try again are packed into chapter 7. You'll discover new ways to think about these setbacks, and yourself, that will help you navigate these inevitable challenges.

PRACTICING SELF-LOVE

Adventure tales often end with the main character recognizing their strength and reconnecting with those around them with greater depth, ease, and appreciation. In short, they have greater self-love, and greater love of others as well. Similarly, this book ends with a chapter on self-love. Trust me when I say that self-love is already inside you. It's very likely what led you to pick up this book in the first place.

It may be hard to believe that self-love is what launched you on this journey. Maybe you were lost, like Dorothy was, or your home had been destroyed, like Luke's had. Or maybe you realized that your quiet, cozy life in the Shire was about to come to an end if you didn't accept the invitation to grow. That's okay. Self-preservation is a form of self-love, and it gets us through the bleakest chapters of our story. But in the last chapter, we'll turn to a kind of self-love oriented toward self-expression rather than self-preservation. Chapter 8 will guide you in exercises that will help you practice self-love with greater awareness and compassion than you ever thought possible.

What to Expect When Working through This Book

Almost universally, human beings struggle with change, even if the change is positive. Paradoxically, positive change can be emotionally challenging, but any change requires the body to adapt in some way. This adaptation response, which involves the release of hormones and neurotransmitters, is known as stress, and any new situation, even a great new situation, is a stressor. Because stressors trigger the release of neurotransmitters, it is common to have an emotional response to stress. If you have a few emotional hiccups while writing your new story of an even better you, you are in great company.

Not all stress is created equal. Sometimes stress is experienced as dreadful, and at other times it's exciting. What makes the difference between good stress and bad stress? As it turns out, whether stress is good or bad is in the eye of the beholder. It is my deep hope that simply knowing that change brings stress, and that how you experience stress has a lot to do with how you think about it, will prepare you to embrace any stress as a sign that you're already succeeding in your change journey. If you weren't, you wouldn't be stressed.

Some of the emotions that you might feel include nervousness, anxiety, and perhaps grumpiness. However, you can choose to experience these emotions as excitement. Remorse, sadness, and even grief are often part of the normal process of personal growth. You might feel a little down, or you could interpret that lower energy state as a sign that you're releasing a burden. It's all right to experience some negative emotions; much of the time this means that you are right on track.

It's expected that uncomfortable feelings will be part of the story. Some of the exercises you'll encounter along the way were designed specifically to help you navigate emotional challenges. Some of them will help you release emotions more easily, and others will teach you how to use these emotions to better understand yourself. Still other exercises will allow you to view these emotions and their triggers differently so you'll experience less distress when they arise.

When feelings emerge along the way, try not to worry about them; most will eventually pass. You can take a break whenever you need to, journal about what you're feeling, or even skip the exercise for now.

Sometimes, however, emotions don't pass, and they might even start to interfere with your normal functioning. Some people might find it difficult to sleep, eat, get to work, or experience joyfulness. When emotions start to interfere with your normal functioning, they become symptoms of a larger problem rather than experiences typical of a change process. If you experience any of these symptoms, you'll want to seek out a therapist or psychiatrist who can help you through these sticky issues. See this book's Resources section for how to find help if needed.

Act Like the Person You Want to Be, Even if You're Not Yet

Do you remember what it was like to learn to tie your shoe or draw a picture? Most likely, you learned these skills so far in your past that you don't remember. But perhaps you do remember being taught how to ride a bike or to swim or some other skill for the first time. Maybe you felt a little scared that first time, and you weren't sure if you would ever *really* feel natural at it. But in time and with practice, your movements became steadier and more fluid. And now, even after years of not doing that activity, you can hop right back into it, and it's just like, well, riding a bike!

Learning anything new can be difficult. You may feel a little uncomfortable in your skin at first. You may think you'll never be any good at this. But, just like when you learned to read, speak, ride a bike, or master another skill, those thoughts are incorrect. Over time, just as when you learn anything else, you'll get better at your new skills and more comfortable with your new habits and traits with continued practice. To continue with the metaphor of writing a new story, practicing your new skills is a bit like the editing process. No writer sits down and gets every word perfect the first time. There are many drafts, some of which are very rough, before the story is ready for publication.

Eventually, this new way of being will feel familiar, comfortable, and authentic. In the meantime, act as if you're the person you want to be, the very best version of yourself. Maybe you've heard the saying "Fake it till you make it." My friend Rev. Pedro Silva offers an even better version: "Be it till you see it." What he's getting at is that we all have the capacity to be wonderful human beings, even if we have developed less-than-great habits. When we want to change how we show up in the world, we may feel like we're faking it at first. Then we come to realize that if we didn't have the potential to behave that way, we wouldn't even be able to fake it. We finally *see* that we've always had the potential to be the person we've wanted to become.

You may notice that these examples focus on feeling more confident with your new skills, not on feeling more confident so that others will be impressed with you. One important note about "acting as if": It's only effective when you're trying to change your internal experience of yourself. If you're "acting as if" for the purpose of changing how *others* view you, the plan is likely to backfire.

I'll discuss more about how to "be it till you see it" in greater detail in chapters 4 and 5. For now, it's enough to know that "acting as if" is a time-tested strategy that can help you as you write a new story of you.

Key Takeaways

- Self-growth is a lifelong process of becoming able to navigate the many changes that life brings our way, such as being able to handle more stress while experiencing less anxiety, handling challenging relationships with less anger, or recovering from setbacks with less despair.

- We can think of the self-growth process as being similar to writing a new story of you. The steps in the self-growth process align nicely with the three-act structure of great stories. Act 1, otherwise known as "the setup," is presented in chapter 3 as you review your past and learn who you are and why. Chapter 4 is also part of act 1; there, you'll identify the goal that drives your new story forward. Act 2, often referred to as "the confrontation," occurs as you take action toward your goal and encounter obstacles along the way. Chapters 5, 6, and 7 will help you grow through these challenges. Act 3, "the resolution," is where you'll experience lasting connection with yourself and others, described in chapter 8.

- You'll likely experience a wide range of emotions while working your way through the exercises in this book. Some of these feelings will help you maintain a positive outlook. But if you become overwhelmed despite your best efforts, see the Resources at the end of the book.

- Your best self is waiting inside you for the right circumstances to emerge. The exercises in this book will help you "be it till you see it" for yourself.

*The understanding of life begins
with the understanding
of pattern.*

—FRITJOF CAPRA

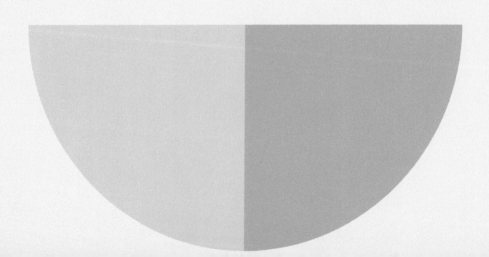

CHAPTER 3

Take an Honest Look at Yourself and Your Past

The new story of you will begin in the way of all stories: with a brief exploration of your character's past. What values inspire you? What strengths can you rely on as you encounter the challenges that will come in this adventure you're about to undertake? What were the major influences that shaped your character?

This chapter will help you home in on who you are at your core by inviting you to explore your core values, identify your superpowers, and reflect on your past to identify patterns in your relationships. You'll have an opportunity to identify your self-limiting beliefs and transform them into uplifting self-liberating beliefs that will see you through this period of change.

Passed Over for Promotion

"I just got passed over for a promotion. A friend of mine in another department recommended life coaching to help me get promoted the next time an upper-level management position opens up," Michael wrote on his intake paperwork.

At our first session, Michael was stunned that he was passed over for promotion. He took responsibility for all the details on every project he worked on. He worked late every night fixing other people's mistakes, and he never bothered his boss with stupid questions. He didn't waste time chatting with coworkers, but instead focused on getting the job done efficiently. He wowed everyone with every presentation he gave.

"I've been at this job for the last nine years," Michael said. "I don't understand why I'm not making it to upper management. I work harder than anyone."

Michael had ended up in a small job market with few options in his pay range. Finding another job in his area seemed unlikely. His wife worried that moving would be hard on their three children. Besides, she had a job she loved. How much money did they need, anyway? Couldn't he just be happy with his current job and maybe work a little less?

When Michael was growing up, his father had owned a chain of furniture stores. His father was a stern man who was seldom home, and he was always in command. Michael's parents were stingy with praise and seemed burdened by his needs for attention and help with his schoolwork. He felt as though he could never please them.

Michael's belief that he was a disappointment to his parents became even stronger when he failed out of college his first year because of test anxiety. "My dad was so ashamed he couldn't even look at me," he said.

THE STORY THE STORY TELLS

After doing a series of exercises like those in this chapter, Michael came to understand himself and the world around him differently. He became acquainted with various parts of himself, some that were afraid of failure and others that saw asking for help as a weakness.

Still other parts of Michael realized his previously unrecognized self-limiting belief: that he was not good enough. This part drove him to take over projects as a way of overcompensating for his imagined short-comings. The part that believed he was inadequate made it hard for him to ask for help at work or even allow his colleagues to contribute to projects. He realized that this also affected his relationships at home. The part that believed he was inadequate made Michael avoid being home so that his family wouldn't see his shortcomings.

Michael finally saw the patterns that had caused him problems, and he immediately learned skills for coping with the anxiety caused by his feelings of inadequacy. After clarifying his values, he had a clear sense of how to move forward. Rather than being hijacked by the parts that held self-limiting beliefs, he was able to maintain a solid connection with what the IFS model refers to as "Self-energy." As a result, he was increasingly able to respond creatively to challenges he faced throughout his growth process. Armed with a clearer sense of who he was and what mattered to him, he was able to chart a path toward a more fulfilling life.

"When you said I was going to have to take an honest look at myself, I was scared," Michael said after several sessions. "I thought I was going to find out that I really *am* a failure. But instead, now I can see my strengths, which helps me accept my weaknesses without feeling hopeless."

To Grow, You Must First Examine Who You Are

Act 1 of your personal growth process will give you an overview of the motivation behind your thoughts, words, and deeds. You'll identify overall patterns that you've been living out. These patterns will reveal *choice points*: one or two places where you might experience a different outcome if you do just one thing differently next time.

We'll begin with a mindfulness exercise. Mindfulness is a powerful tool for managing challenging emotions without being overwhelmed by them. That's because mindfulness helps you tap into that core Self-energy that the IFS model says is at the core of every human. When you operate from that fully resourced place within yourself, you'll have what it takes to write a new story of you instead of becoming discouraged by the old one.

Exploring values and identifying your strengths show you the "why" of your character. Your values will become your navigational equipment throughout the remainder of this book. When you're at those choice points, rather than acting out of habit, you can begin to act in alignment with your values instead of acting out of habit. Your strengths will become the superpowers you use to resolve conflicts that arise in act 2 of your story, when obstacles and challenges arise.

The "why" of your character will become clearer as you survey important relationships and developments in your history. For many of us, this is the most challenging part of the process. This survey commonly stirs up painful emotions in the present. Take this exercise slowly, use your new mindfulness skills (which you'll learn in the first exercise), and be gentle with yourself. You'll have a clear sense of your stuck places and self-limiting beliefs, which will empower you to change them.

Self-limiting beliefs typically result from negative experiences. These beliefs tend to be extreme and rigid. For example, someone who was yelled at for spilling milk when they were a child may develop the belief "I can't do anything right." This belief is extreme in that it takes one fault and makes it the whole story. It is also rigid: It hasn't changed despite significant evidence to the contrary, as anyone who has survived to adulthood has done many things right.

Finally, you'll create antidotes to the self-limiting beliefs that have been holding you back. These will take the form of positive thoughts about yourself that you can agree with and believe in. I'll suggest some, and you'll create others. When you've collected a set of antidotes that feels complete, you'll use them in a variety of ways to guide the plot as you continue to write this exciting new story of you.

As with all exercises, be sure that you're in a space where you feel physically and emotionally safe to try something new. Respect the limits of your mind, body, and spirit, and pause if you need to. Each exercise builds on the one before it, so you'll get more out of this chapter if you do them in order. Take all the time you need.

1. MINDFULNESS ACTIVITY: GETTING CENTERED

Practice this meditation for five minutes each day with your eyes open. You'll build new neural pathways that will help you navigate the change process. Try recording yourself reading the steps, and play it back while you meditate.

1. Find a comfortable seat where you can put your feet flat on the floor if you are able to.

2. Take a deep breath in and release it to the count of four, noticing how your body responds as you do it.

3. Notice where your body makes contact with the chair or the ground beneath your feet. Feel your body being supported.

4. As you exhale, release any uncomfortable energy through those points of contact, sending it down to the earth below.

5. Look slowly around the room, turning your neck as far as you can to each side. Look as far up and as far down as you can. Move slowly and comfortably.

6. What do you notice in the space you're in? What catches the light? What beauty do you see?

7. Use this exercise any time you feel your emotions start to get the better of you, especially if negative thoughts or emotions arise as you're completing the exercises in this book.

● ● ● ● 2. FINDING YOUR INNER COMPASS ● ● ● ●

Review the following list of values. Circle fifteen to twenty of them that you see yourself living out in your daily life. Feel free to write in and circle any values you hold that don't appear on the list.

Acceptance	Gratitude	Productivity
Adventure	Growth	Reliability
Awareness	Happiness	Renewal
Balance	Harmony	Resourcefulness
Beauty	Health	Security
Bravery	Honesty	Service
Calm	Humor	Spontaneity
Commitment	Individuality	Strength
Community	Joy	Thoughtfulness
Compassion	Justice	Understanding
Confidence	Kindness	Trustworthiness
Connection	Knowledge	Wisdom
Creativity	Leadership	
Curiosity	Learning	_____
Dependability	Love	
Dignity	Loyalty	_____
Discipline	Maturity	
Empathy	Mindfulness	_____
Fairness	Openness	
Faith	Patience	_____
Friendship	Peace	
Generosity	Play	_____

Review the words you circled and put a star next to your top five most important values, those that you couldn't possibly do without. These are your headline values. Write them in the top row of the table on the next page.

Then record your remaining values in the second row of the table, sorting them into value clusters that align with your most important values. (For example, if a top five value is "renewal," you might write your remaining values of "adventure," "balance," and "mindfulness" in the value cluster for it.)

Your Top Value Clusters

••• 3. IDENTIFYING YOUR SUPERPOWERS •••

Ask three to five of your closest friends, family members, or coworkers what they think are your top three strengths. Also ask them for evidence that you show that strength. Reflect on their responses.

1. Based on the feedback from others as well as your own self-reflection, what are your top three strengths?

   _____

2. What do you do on a regular basis that reflects or requires those strengths?

   _____

3. How do those strengths show up in your social/professional relationships?

   _____

4. How do those strengths show up in your romantic relationships?

   _____

5. How might you use those strengths to reach your personal growth goals (for example, dating, career, spiritual growth, wellness)? Be very specific.

   _____

Now that you've located your inner compass, you can create an inspiriting statement that summarizes what you've learned so far:

I am a person of _____

_____ (top three strengths).

I am bringing more _____

_____ (top three values) into the world.

Heroes may be young or old, rich or poor, earthling or alien, but one thing almost all of them have in common is being plagued with self-doubt at some point in their story. You may also be struggling with self-limiting beliefs. The key to overcoming these beliefs is to recognize them for what they are. Major indicators of self-limiting beliefs are:

- They take an all-or-nothing approach.

- They make you feel awful inside.

- They portray things as unchanging.

Self-limiting beliefs often have their roots in our worst experiences, such as harsh words from parents, embarrassing situations in school, or betrayals by friends and partners. These beliefs are held by those protectors we talked about before, and their whole intention is to prevent pain. However, because parts don't see the big picture, they might disregard information that could be even more helpful at preventing pain. For example, self-limiting beliefs do not account for our successes or achievements, or the people who have been helpful to us. As a result, we don't see a balanced picture.

Here are the key things to keep in mind when creating antidotes to reduce the venomous effects of such thoughts:

- Make them uplifting so that when you read them, you feel inspired.

- Keep your antidotes believable; focusing on your values, strengths, or accomplishments will help you believe them.

- Repeat them often. Research has shown that the unsupervised mind tends toward negative thinking. You'll need to be intentional about moving your thoughts in a more positive direction.

You'll have an opportunity to identify your own self-limiting beliefs and create tailor-made antidotes later in this chapter.

These questions will help you think about how you'll frame your own story. You'll examine what has shaped you into the person you are. There's a lot to consider, so take the time you need to reflect on and answer these questions, or come back to them later.

1. What parts of your personality do you feel most proud of?

2. What parts of yourself do you most feel you need to hide when you're around others?

3. What successes and accomplishments are you most proud of?

4. Reflecting on past romantic relationships, what patterns do you notice around the types of people you attract and the problems that arise?

5. What challenges tend to recur in workplace relationships?

6. What emotional needs do your friends meet? How do you feel around your friends?

7. What do you remember about the relationship your parents had with each other (including stepparents)? What did you learn about love from witnessing their interactions?

8. Describe your relationship with your parents. Which of your needs were met or unmet? Did you receive the affection, attention, nurturing, and love that you needed?

9. How did your parents or caregivers celebrate your successes and navigate your failures?

10. Looking back, how would you summarize the story about your current struggles?

_____

_____

• • • • • • • • • • 5. IDENTIFYING YOUR • • • • • • • • •
SELF-LIMITING BELIEFS

The following is a list of common self-limiting beliefs. Which ones come up for you? Circle them, then move onto the next exercise and create antidotes for the poison they carry.

1. Everything I've tried fails.
2. I don't deserve success.
3. I don't know how to change.
4. I just don't have it in me to change.
5. I'll never amount to anything.
6. I'm a bad person.
7. I'm a failure.
8. I'm not worthy of happiness.
9. I'm too lazy to change.
10. I'm too old to change.
11. I'm unlovable.
12. I'm worthless.
13. My problems are too big for me to handle.

14. No one can be trusted.
15. No one likes me.
16. Nothing ever works out for me.
17. Only weaklings ask for help.
18. People don't change.
19. There's no point in trying.

What other self-limiting beliefs do you hold?

_____

_____

_____

_____

_____

• • • • • • • • 6. CREATING ANTIDOTES TO • • • • • • • • SELF-LIMITING BELIEFS

In exercises 2 to 4, you collected evidence of your strengths, values, and successes. In this exercise, you'll use this evidence to create antidotes (positive statements or affirmations about yourself) to your self-limiting beliefs.

Based on this evidence, write positive statements or affirmations that reinforce these strengths. Here are some ideas to get you started:

I lean on my intelligence, humor, and adaptability to help me grow.
I stand for integrity.

- I'm proud of _____ (your response to exercise 4, question 1).

- I have succeeded at _____ (your response to exercise 4, question 3).

- I lean on _____ (your response to exercise 3, question 1) to help me grow.

- Today, I stand for _____ (Value Clusters, exercise 2).

- I'm becoming the best version of myself.

- I'm committed to building on my strengths.

- I'm committed to learning from all of my experiences.

Now try writing five positive statements or affirmations of your own:

1. _____

_____

2. _____

_____

3. _____

_____

4. _____

_____

5. _____

_____

Recite these positive statements to yourself several times a day. Write them on sticky notes and post them where you'll see them often: a mirror, a door, the refrigerator. Save them on your phone or computer screensaver/wallpaper. Create a drawing, painting, or other artwork. Write them in your daily journal.

Key Takeaways

- Personal growth requires you to take a close look at yourself and your past. If you're looking closely, you should be able to identify what you're proud of and your dearest values and strengths that are already helping you in your daily life. You may also discover patterns of behavior that aren't serving you.

- There are many ways to stop the negative behaviors that currently affect you. Simply stopping them isn't enough, though, because you'll run the risk of substituting another behavior that also may not be helpful (for example, eating potato chips instead of smoking). The best approach is to orient yourself toward the values that will help you thrive. Acting, thinking, and speaking in a way that aligns with and expresses your values will lead you to deep fulfillment.

- The patterns you identified in exercise 4 are changeable to an extent. You can't change others, but you can change your own approach to interactions, which changes everything.

- Self-limiting beliefs are your mind's way of trying to protect you by minimizing risk. However, to grow and change, you'll have to take some well-considered risks. Creating antidotes to your self-limiting beliefs will help you develop the courage to do what's necessary to create a life you love. The best way to do this is to create an uplifting statement that you can believe in, and to repeat it often.

- With practice, you'll make decisions that align with and reflect your values rather than your fears or your worst thoughts about yourself and others.

Define your own goals regardless
of what others think or say.

—JAMES O. PROCHASKA,
JOHN C. NORCROSS, AND
CARLO C. DICLEMENTE

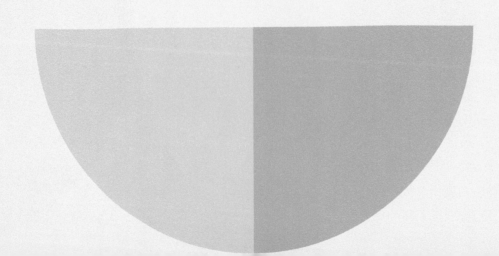

CHAPTER 4

Setting Goals with a Purpose

Why does the hero take on the enormous challenge set before them? Act 1 helps us understand why the hero is willing to set off for adventure despite the risks. What is it about their background that leads them to this situation? Knowing what's a stake for the hero, we become invested in their success, too

Similarly, you'll be more energized to reach your change goals if you're clear on your reason for change . Adventure heroes are often motivated by fear of ultimate evil. We're taking a more positive approach, though, so this chapter will guide you to anchor your motivation in your highest aspirations for self-fulfillment. The exercises will help you clarify your vision for the future and your reasons for achieving it. You'll also have an opportunity to think through all that you'll want to pack in your satchel as you set off on the adventure of change.

Purpose Fuels Change

"I positively hate my job, and it's making me hate the rest of my life, too. I want to quit, but I don't know what else to do," Sue told her life coach during her first visit.

Sue is a success by anyone's standard. At forty-three, she is a physician and happily married with preteen twins. But despite all that, she still feels unfulfilled.

Sue became a doctor to make her mother happy. Although her mother passed away some time ago, Sue still feels obligated to continue in her current career. Her family counts on her to earn a big paycheck. Her patients trust her for their medical care. And the partners at her medical practice count on her to do her share of the workload.

Sue hired a life coach because she knew she needed support and guidance in making a career change. She ended her first few coaching sessions with good intentions to complete the homework she agreed to. But week after week, she kept forgetting to do the agreed-on exercise.

"What gets in the way of meeting your accountability goals?" her coach asked.

"Well, you know, the usual. Work, housework, spending time with the kids," Sue replied. "And gosh, this is so embarrassing, but I've also been spending a lot of time playing games on my phone."

"I see that you're serious about making a change, but I also see that there's another part getting in the way. What can you tell me about that part?" her coach asked.

"Well, yes. Part of me does want to change. But another part is really scared of the unknown, and it sort of shuts me down," Sue said.

THE STORY THE STORY TELLS

Sue names what prevents most people from changing: fear. It may be fear of the unknown, fear of failure, fear of success. If you're feeling fearful, you're not alone. Heroes in every great adventure story encounter fear at some point of their story, often in the very beginning. Whether they must find their way home, defeat Darth Vader, or destroy the One Ring, they ask themselves, "How could someone like me do this?" In the end, their self-limiting fearful beliefs are almost always proved wrong, and it's very likely that yours will be, too.

Sue had been shutting down instead of doing her coaching homework, but she had also been shutting down way before then. She was playing games on her phone to the point where many important daily tasks weren't getting done. She was eating fast food instead of cooking healthy meals, she was emotionally unavailable to her family, and she wasn't exercising.

She had plunged into coaching, and the change process in general, before deeply connecting with her motivation for change. As a result, fear of change continued to keep her from even getting started. Our first goal was to help Sue firmly connect to the "why" behind her decision to change. What potential benefit lay on the other side of this change process? What might it feel like to experience true fulfillment? The excitement she experienced with this vision in mind energized her, but it still wasn't quite enough.

Next, we worked to clarify the cost of *not* changing, which was recently revealed: Sue was experiencing early signs of diabetes. By deeply considering the impact of diabetes on herself and her family members, Sue recognized that the benefits of change far outweighed any other risk she might face during the growth process. She was also able to see that worries about finances were a smokescreen for her fears of change.

Goals with Purpose Are More Likely to Succeed

Inertia is the inability to get moving. We've all experienced the kind of fear that shuts you down. It doesn't feel like fear, though; it feels gray, boring, heavy, and uninspired. That's the kind of fear that kept Sue from succeeding in her plans to change, and maybe it has done the same to you in the past.

There's also another kind of fear, one that's more energizing and leads you to take action. Everyone knows what being energized feels like: It's hard to sit still, and you feel a bodily need to *do* something. Both excitement and the energized feeling caused by fear originate in the same part of your nervous system.

Epic adventure stories always tap into both excitement and energizing fear. The hero is motivated because rising to the challenge set before them will bring them something of value. Dorothy will return to her family. Luke will become a Jedi and conquer evil. Frodo will protect the Shire from Sauron. Heroes are also motivated by the energizing fear that if they don't act, something awful will happen—something even more awful than the discomfort of change.

The twin thoughts of the fate that awaits the hero if they don't forge ahead and the rewards they will receive at the end of the journey don't just get the hero moving; they *keep* them moving even when circumstances are tough. The hero in these stories knows precisely what is at stake in the adventure, and no matter how hard it gets, they can reconnect with the purpose that inspired them in the first place.

In this chapter and the next, you'll encounter several exercises designed to help you tap into both excitement and energizing fear. Through visualizations, storytelling, and creative projects, you'll develop excitement about the benefits of achieving your goals. By connecting these goals with your dearest values (discovered in chapter 3), you'll connect your personal story of change to a deeper purpose. You'll also discover that the behaviors and thoughts you're working to change are not at all aligned with your deeply held values.

You'll move from the first kind of fear (the kind that shuts you down) toward the kind of fear that gets you moving by countering your self-limiting beliefs and identifying the cost of *not* changing. You'll have an opportunity to consider the cost of not changing to yourself, to your family, and to others whom you love.

Additionally, you'll fill in a bit more of the backstory of yourself as hero. You'll get a thumbnail sketch of the knowledge, skills, and habits of mind required to make the changes you're contemplating. You'll identify what's needed, and you'll make a plan to acquire those things. You'll learn to set SMART goals in preparation for the exercises in chapter 6 (see page 59). Altogether, these exercises offer an opportunity for you to connect deeply to your purpose for change, inspiring you to get moving and stay moving as you dive into your new story of you.

••••• 1. TWELVE MONTHS FROM NOW •••••

This exercise will help you get a clear feeling imprint of your ideal personal or professional situation. First, review exercises 2 and 3 in chapter 3, then read through the instructions for this visualization. It may help you focus if you record yourself reading the following questions so that you are free to imagine.

Find a quiet spot where you can sit for about fifteen minutes undisturbed. Take a comfortable seat and allow your eyes to close. Imagine what your life will be like twelve months from now if you're successful in rewriting your story of you.

How will you relate to close friends or family now that you are your best self? How do you see them benefiting from you living your values, using your strengths, and leading from self? How does it feel to add to their lives in this way?

What do you feel inside as you imagine expressing your values and using your strengths more effectively in a professional setting? What new opportunities do you see?

Imagine looking back at your growth process from the position of having already met your goals. What did it take to succeed? How did your strengths help?

Now that you've done the visualization in exercise 2, take a few moments to reflect on the experience. Grab a notebook and pen (or open a Word document) and write down your responses to the prompts that follow.

In your visualization:

How does it feel to have a life that is such a good fit for your strengths and values?

_____

_____

_____

How does it feel to operate from your best self?

_____

_____

_____

What are the major benefits you're experiencing by changing?

_____

_____

_____

How are family and friends benefiting from the changes?

_____

_____

_____

What are you doing in your new life to better express the values you identified in chapter 3, exercise 2?

_____

_____

_____

How are you using your strengths, as identified in chapter 3, exercise 3, to help you create change?

_____

_____

_____

What changes in your personal or professional life support greater expression of your values and increased self-leadership?

_____

_____

_____

How does being self-led, values-based, and strength-oriented support your financial values and goals, as well as your major personal goals?

_____

_____

_____

•••••• 3. GET WISE TO YOUR "WHYS" ••••••

The following are some common benefits that people experience when making big changes in their lives. Circle the three potential benefits that most inspire you and add any others that come to mind.

☐ A job I am more passionate about

☐ Better relationship with my part-ner, significant other, or spouse

☐ Better sleep

☐ Closer friendships

☐ Feeling healthier

☐ Feeling of purpose

☐ Happiness

☐ Improved appearance

☐ Improved reputation

☐ Increased confidence

☐ Less anxiety

☐ Less conflict at work

☐ Less stress

☐ Make a bigger contribution to the world

☐ More energy for fun

☐ More freedom

☐ More likely to get a raise/promotion

☐ More popular

☐ Pride

☐ Service to community

☐ Setting a better example for my children

☐ Other:

☐ _____

☐ _____

What makes the benefits you selected (or wrote in) so important to you?

_____

_____

_____

_____

_____

How might you feel if you don't make these changes within the next year or so?

_____

_____

_____

_____

_____

How can you remind yourself every day of what you're working to achieve?

_____

_____

_____

_____

_____

SELF-LIMITING BELIEFS

During the early stages of your change journey, it's common to experience specific types of self-limiting beliefs that can derail you.

"I'll start tomorrow."

Procrastination commonly occurs early in the change process. To some degree, success *does* depend on timing, so this isn't all bad. Successful change requires taking the time to prepare. You prepare by evaluating the ways that your new story of you better aligns with your values, identifying the costs of your current thoughts and actions, and acquiring the skills needed to change.

"I'm going to surprise everyone with the new, improved me."

Keeping private about your plans to change undermines your commitment and cuts you off from the support you might receive from friends and family. There's something about going public with your desire for change that leads you to become more invested in success. When you talk about your commitment and your motivations, it's likely that your friends and family will also invest in your success, just like what happens in the adventure stories I keep mentioning.

"It's not my fault I'm like this."

Shifting blame makes it much less likely that a person will successfully change. If something isn't your fault, how can you be expected to change it? The problem is, no one else can change it for you.

"It's no big deal."

Minimizing the problems caused by the thoughts and behaviors you're interested in changing is a rationalization: a way of talking yourself out of change.

All of these self-limiting beliefs are caused by fear. Change is scary. To successfully change, you'll need to come up with reasons that are powerful enough to outweigh your fears. This chapter will help you find those reasons.

•••• 4. KEEPING YOUR VISION IN MIND ••••

Notice how good it feels to imagine being on the other side of these changes. It's uplifting, isn't it? If you can dream it, you can do it. But between now and the moment you reach the end of the story, you'll have moments of doubt.

To keep yourself inspired along the way, create a vision board that will help you connect with the good feelings generated in exercise 1, chapter 4.

Have a look through some magazines and search online for images that trigger feelings similar to those that arose during the visualization exercise. These images should not only trigger those good feelings, but they should also allow you to easily connect what you see with the goals you're working toward. You can also collect words or phrases that speak to the changes you're making.

Once you've collected images, words, and phrases, you can create a collage. Tape or glue these images and words to poster board, paper, or just to each other.

Hang the collage somewhere you'll see it daily. Throughout your change process, take a few seconds every day to glance at it and reconnect with the wonderful feelings you'll have once you reach your goal.

• • • • • • • • • • 5. MIND THE GAP • • • • • • • • • •

Not a single hero in any adventure story ever achieved their goal without training or support. Heroes typically stumble into a guide or teacher who tells them what they need. Similarly, you may have to fill in a few gaps in your knowledge, skills, and habits of mind to successfully live out your new story of you. Here, you'll become your own guide and teacher.

Grab a piece of paper or open a Word document and brainstorm at least five to ten answers to the following questions. You're about to do what is known in the business world as a SWOT analysis (SWOT is an acronym that stands for "strength, weakness, opportunity, threat").

What strengths do you already have that will help you achieve your change goals? Think in terms of personal characteristics, resources, relationships, knowledge, and so on.

What weaknesses or deficiencies must be addressed to help you achieve your change goals?

What opportunities exist in your environment to support your change goals? Examples are smoking-cessation programs, Overeaters Anonymous meetings, and resources at the local library.

_____

_____

_____

_____

_____

What threats in your environment will you have to navigate? Examples might be a nearby bakery, heavy work demands, or a living situation you share with a smoker.

_____

_____

_____

_____

_____

• • • • • • • • • 6. SET SMART GOALS • • • • • • • • •

Until now, we've described your change goals in vague terms. Let's get your goals into sharper focus.

SMART stands for "specific, measurable, achievable, realistic, and time-bound." You'll also want to consider your why for your goals.

Can you identify the SMART goals in this list?

1. Lisa tells her friends she wants to lose ten pounds this week because she's getting married in a month.

2. Ramón commits to reducing his anger outbursts to zero per week within three months because they strain family relationships.

3. Ty tells his supervisor that he'll be more polite to customers because he wants a raise.

4. Angela hopes she'll overcome her shyness and go to her friend's party next weekend because she doesn't want to hurt her friend's feelings.

5. Elaine intends to find a new job with a 10 percent increase in pay within six months because she wants to increase her retirement savings.

6. Dan says he'll quit smoking tomorrow because he wants to be healthier.

If you identified 2, 4, and 5, you have a very clear sense of how to write SMART goals. Now try writing your own:

Specific: _____

_____

_____

_____

Measurable: _____

_____

_____

_____

Achievable: _____

_____

_____

_____

Time-bound: _____

_____

_____

_____

Your "why": _____

_____

_____

_____

Key Takeaways

- The number one reason most people don't change is the fear of the unknown. A dismal status quo often feels more comfortable than taking steps to improve the situation. That's because we can't always be sure what lies on the other side of the change we're considering. If you find yourself procrastinating, hiding your plans to change from people close to you, or making excuses for why a particular problem isn't so bad, check in with yourself. Fear is usually lurking underneath.

- Reinforce your commitment to change and ensure that your changes feel meaningful to you. It's important to consider how the changes you're considering will help your thoughts, words, and deeds come into better alignment with your top values, discovered in chapter 3. If they're not, how will the changes you're considering express your values more effectively?

- Research the true cost of *not* changing. If you don't stop smoking, what are the health risks? If you continue to let fears and worries keep you from a career change, what is the potential loss of income and joy? If you're not sure, do some research.

- Consider your stakeholders: friends and family who love you and coworkers and bosses who depend on you. How might they benefit from the changes you're considering?

- How will you reconnect with the deep purpose motivating your changes when you encounter challenges? A vision board or collage, or another creative project, can be helpful.

Once the commitment is made to change, it is time to move.

**—JAMES O. PROCHASKA,
JOHN C. NORCROSS, AND
CARLO C. DICLEMENTE**

CHAPTER 5

Taking Action and Forming the Habits You Want

We've finally come to act 2 of our story: the confrontation. Here, you'll take powerful steps toward your goals. It's time to *do* things differently, not simply imagine them. Just like those other heroes are tested during the confrontation, you, too, will be tested. The key to passing these tests is preparation, which is the early stage of the change process. Most of the changes that occur during this stage are taking place on the inside.

This chapter will help you with your final preparations by showing you how to get in touch with the various parts of your personality that may be blocking your path. You'll have the opportunity to identify your kryptonite (behaviors, people, circumstances, and thoughts that may prove to be poisonous to your change process) and create antidotes to it. The final exercise will help you affirm your commitment to yourself by guiding you through your first action step.

It Starts Today . . . or Does It?

"That's it! My new exercise routine starts right now," Jack announced to his family the day his father suffered a mild heart attack. His father's health emergency jolted Jack out of his denial. A lifetime of bacon-and-egg breakfasts and steak dinners, combined with a sedentary lifestyle, had led to his father's heart condition. Jack was heading in the same direction, given his similar diet. Suddenly, Jack's fear of disease overrode his fear of change, energizing him for action.

Standing at his father's bedside, Jack thought he would be motivated enough to make these changes last for the rest of his life. If he didn't have the willpower to change after that, it was his own fault, he decided.

As the owner of a small business, Jack was used to going it alone, and he believed in the importance of willpower. He was pretty sure he could manage changing his eating habits. All it takes is commitment, he thought.

Because of Jack's heavy work demands, his partner, Paul, had taken on full responsibility for grocery shopping. Paul was happy to cook low-fat meals, but he didn't see the problem with buying cakes, cookies, and other baked goods. After all, it was Jack's diet, not Paul's. Also, Jack typically bought donuts for his employees twice a week as a morale builder. He didn't want to disappoint them. "What harm could there be in buying them donuts? I don't have to eat them," Jack thought. So he continued stopping at the bakery on the way to work twice a week.

Two weeks into Jack's new diet, his business lost a major client, and the stress became overwhelming. It eroded Jack's willpower, and he couldn't suppress the urge to stress-eat. He found himself devouring a donut that afternoon.

A week later, only three weeks after his decision to change his diet, Jack was back to his former eating habits.

THE STORY THE STORY TELLS

Jack's story reveals the pitfalls common in act 2 of great adventure stories. The hero tries to go it alone and fails. Or the hero tries to use their super-power but finds that their enemy has a way of getting around it, like Lex Luthor's use of kryptonite with Superman. In every great adventure story is a moment when it seems unlikely that the hero will succeed.

You may have that same experience in your own change journey, but there are several steps you can take to ensure that you're more successful making your change than Jack was his first time around.

After visiting with a wellness coach, Jack learned that he'd launched into his new lifestyle with a few misconceptions. He imagined that the magic moment at his father's bedside would make a lasting impression. He thought change was simply a matter of willpower, so it wasn't necessary to create or follow a plan. And because the changes he wanted to make were, in his mind, a matter of life and death, he couldn't imagine not receiving the support he needed. Underneath it all, Jack realized that he'd been afraid to appear weak, and he couldn't ask for help.

Through coaching, Jack recognized that Paul's continued purchasing of cookies and cakes was undermining Jack's commitment to change. Jack *did* need help, and he needed to develop the courage and humility to ask for it.

He also learned that he would benefit from using tools other than sheer willpower. Jack asked his partner for support, learned several stress-management techniques, started purchasing fresh fruit platters for the office instead of donuts, and began practicing an exercise routine to support his commitment to change. He also did some work with the parts of himself that were skeptical or afraid of change.

Within weeks, Jack was well on his way to lasting change.

All Change Begins with Action

If you want different results, you need to take different actions. But as it turns out, not all actions are equally valuable. The kinds of actions that lead to lasting change are typically gradual and well supported. What does that mean? Well, if your change goal is to stop swearing, you'll want to cut back a little at a time rather than expecting yourself to completely stop at once, and you might want to reward yourself for every small success. Perhaps you can put a dollar in a jar for every hour you go without swearing, and then use that money to treat yourself to something special at the end of the week.

You'll need not only your support but also the support of others around you. This is where things can get tricky. Let's say you're trying to eat healthier, but your spouse wants to keep eating pizza and donuts. Your changes will affect them, which might create stress in the relationship.

Change can also create stress even when you're receiving support. That's because one simple change (for example, deciding to improve your anger management skills) often requires other changes. How will you reduce the stress and anxiety that have led you to become so short-tempered in the past? How will you avoid situations that tend to result in irritability, such as working right up to a deadline? You'll need to discover several options to help you manage the stress that arises.

You've already practiced one of the biggest stress relievers in earlier chapters: mindfulness. We've done a mindfulness practice in each chapter as guided imagery, but there are many other mindfulness practices you can use. The Insight Timer and other apps have numerous options. Matthew Rezac's *Mindfulness Activities for Adults* (2021) is also a fantastic resource.

Exercise is another powerful stress reliever. It causes the brain to release chemicals that produce feelings of well-being, and it also helps fill time that perhaps you used to fill with some of those behaviors you're now hoping to change.

Some changes can't be managed without medical assistance or should be undertaken gradually. Quite often, continuing to use even a small amount of a dependency-producing substance makes it even more difficult to quit. In other cases, quitting cold turkey can pose health risks. For example, people who drink heavily can experience seizures or even die if they suddenly stop. If you're struggling to overcome alcohol or substance abuse, please see your health care provider.

The actions you take during act 2 of your new story of you (the confrontation) will be many. You'll enlist the support of friends and family. If you don't have supportive friends and family, you'll research groups and organizations that have the capacity to support your changes. You'll create a list of healthy behaviors that will help you replace the behavior you want to eliminate. The exercises that follow will help you build a solid structure to support your growth.

••••••• **1. MOVING THROUGH FEAR** •••••••

If you're feeling afraid of making changes right now, you're not alone. In fact, that feeling is normal. Your change process will be more effective if you form a better relationship with your fearful parts instead of ignoring them or letting them prevent you from reaching your goals.

If you, like Sue and Jack, are struggling with fearful parts, try this guided imagery.

Find your way into your center, much as you did in exercise 1, chapter 3. Notice where the fearful part resides in your body. Take a moment to sit with it, and let it know you're there with it.

What do you notice about the fearful part? How does it feel? Is it hard or soft? Is it moving or still? Does it feel hot or cold?

Send that fearful part some compassion.

How does that part help you? What is it afraid would happen if it stopped doing its job? What does that part need from you? What would it take for that fearful part to let you be in charge?

Can you agree to do those things?

Now that you're better acquainted with the fearful part, one of many parts you'll encounter on your change journey, you're ready to move on to the next exercise: Parts Mapping.

What thoughts and feelings arise as you consider taking action? Each of these thoughts and feelings can be seen as different parts or characters in your story of you. Some of these parts are in favor of changing and clearly see the benefits, others are actively opposed to changing for a variety of reasons, and still others are undecided and will eventually choose a side later in the change process.

Just like rivals or strangers in an adventure story, parts can be brought together around a shared goal. Think about Dorothy's Tin Man, Cowardly Lion, and Scarecrow, or Aragorn and Boromir in *The Lord of the Rings*. But first, you and your parts have to get acquainted with one another.

Map your own parts in the following diagram, keeping the following questions in mind: Who are these parts as individuals? Where are they in relationship to you? How do they relate to one another? What do they care about? What are their hopes and fears? How can you help them find common ground?

Draw more circles if you need to.

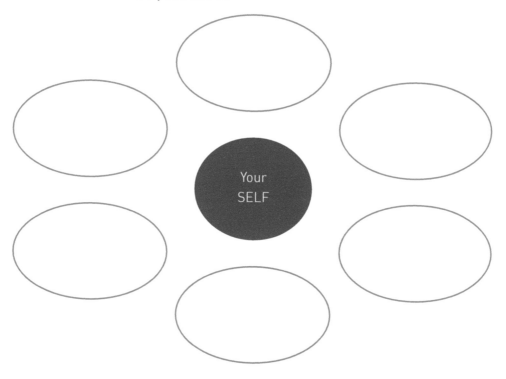

• • • • • • 3. MAKING A COUNTEROFFER • • • • • • •

If you're planning to stop doing something, you'll want to think about what you'd prefer to do instead. Knowing that all change can be stressful, you also need to consider how you'll manage the stress that will come with that change. In other words, you'll want to *counter* your usual behaviors with thoughts and actions that are more aligned with your highest values whenever life presents you with an opportunity to revert to your old ways. Here are a few examples:

When Sharice experiences a midafternoon slump, she usually reaches for a candy bar.
Counteroffer: *Sharice goes for a fifteen-minute walk to reenergize.*

Max usually responds to stress at work by taking a cigarette break.
Counteroffer: *Max decides to take a mindfulness break instead.*

Self-critical thoughts tend to arise whenever Sara tries something new.
Counteroffer: *Sara interrupts self-critical thoughts and congratulates herself for being brave.*

Brainstorm your counteroffers in the spaces that follow. The top three are there as a suggestion since they're so powerful.

Exercise: _____

_____

_____

Mindfulness practices: _____

_____

_____

Antidotes for self-limiting beliefs: _____

_____

_____

SELF-LIMITING BELIEFS

Just as we saw with the example of Jack and his dietary changes, act 2 of your new story of you may feature some new varieties of self-limiting beliefs.

Belief in "magical moments."
Many people are spurred to change by dramatic events in their lives, such as job loss, divorce, illness, or the death of a loved one. These "magical moments" may spur us toward change, but they won't be enough to see us to the other side. To make our changes real, we must practice, struggle, maybe even fail, and then recommit to our best selves once again.

"This should be easy."
Change is much harder than people realize from the outside, even when the changes are good, necessary, and desired. When you're feeling challenged, know you're not alone. Change is hard for everyone.

"Everyone will support me."
No, not everyone will. Some people who love you dearly will be inconvenienced by your new story of you. They'll be challenged to make changes of their own as your relationship shifts. If your changes involve stopping certain behaviors, such as smoking, drinking, or gambling, your new lifestyle will take you away from some of those relationships and may cause those folks who are continuing those same behaviors to feel self-conscious. Don't take any of this personally. Find people who *can* support you on this journey.

One thing at a time.
Take an assertive approach to personal change. Try numerous tools, and use them all at once. No matter what you want to change, add exercise and mindfulness, which will support your sense of well-being. Try techniques that may be outside your comfort zone. I've worked with many people who were too embarrassed to use reminders, affirmations, or self-help groups. They're much less successful than my clients who embrace those practices.

• • • • • • • 4. RESISTANCE TRAINING • • • • • • •

Everyone has their kryptonite, even Superman. Kryptonite for you is anything likely to pose a challenge to your superpowers. Which situations or people currently make it easy for you to continue without changing? Which situations are likely to be overly tempting for you? Which people are likely to pressure you into remaining the same? This exercise asks you to create an antidote to every type of kryptonite you can imagine encountering.

WHAT'S YOUR KRYPTONITE?	WHAT ARE THE ANTIDOTES TO YOUR KRYPTONITE?
Specifically identify situations and people likely to challenge your ability to stay on track with your change process. *Avoid your kryptonite for a while.*	*Identify the places you can go and people you can spend time with to support the changes you're making.* *Invest your time and energy here.*
Spending too much time watching the news	Watch something funny on Netflix
Leo's constant complaining	Spend time painting
I drink too much when I spend time with Britt	Call Jay instead

••••• 5. USE EVERY TOOL IN THE SHED ••••••

When you're tackling ingrained patterns of thought, word, and deed, you'll want to use every possible tool to support your progress, regardless of what your self-limiting beliefs might tell you. The following is a list of tools that many successful self-changers use to help support themselves during act 2 of their new story. Check the ones that speak to you.

☐ Assemble a list of books related to change in general, or your specific changes, and put it into the notes app on your phone, then search your local library or bookstore for those books

☐ Develop a list of skills that you'd like to develop in support of your change

☐ Conduct research into change strategies for the changes you're trying to make

☐ Create a spreadsheet to track change

☐ Create a work of art that will inspire you: collage, painting, pottery

☐ Develop a weekly action plan and post it to a whiteboard

☐ Find a support group (twelve-step, Weight Watchers, etc.)

- ☐ Join a Meetup or Facebook group focused on building the skills and/or environment you need to promote your growth process

- ☐ Journaling

- ☐ Meditation/mindfulness practice

- ☐ Post affirmations around the house

- ☐ Put your list of counteroffers and antidotes for your kryptonite in your phone, wallet, or pocketbook, or post it on the refrigerator

- ☐ Set affirmations as reminders on your phone

- ☐ Set up calendar events to block out time for change-related activities (exercise, mindfulness, etc.)

- ☐ Set up calendar events to check in with yourself about your progress

- ☐ Use a photo of your vision board/collage as your screensaver, lock screen, or desktop wallpaper

- ☐ Write a daily to-do list to keep yourself on track

- ☐ Write a poem or blog post to share your experience

••• 6. MOVING FORWARD COURAGEOUSLY •••

To be completely honest, the fact that you're reading this book is already an action step. You are, right this minute, acquiring knowledge, skills, and habits of mind that will serve you in the process of change. You've been doing so with every exercise you've completed so far. Yes, I know, that was a little sneaky of me to get you to take your first few action steps without you even knowing.

Now it's time to consciously, and with full intention, take your first action step.

1. Choose one tool you circled on the list in exercise 5.

2. Use that tool right now.

Voilà! You've taken your first intentional action step into act 2 of your new story of you.

What can you do to celebrate taking that step?

_____

_____

_____

_____

Why did you choose that action, and how do you see it helping you as you move forward?

_____

_____

_____

_____

How do you feel now that you're aware of all the action steps you've already taken?

_____

_____

_____

_____

Think of another step you can challenge yourself to take in the next twenty-four hours to send yourself a signal that you're fully committed to this change.

_____

_____

_____

_____

Key Takeaways

- Lasting change happens slowly and, in most cases, gradually. You might not get your new thoughts and behaviors perfect right from the beginning. At first, it will be helpful to celebrate each time you *don't* engage in the old behaviors or thoughts, even if your efforts aren't flawless or even smooth. It's about progress, not perfection. You can build on your successes and gradually shape your behavior to align with your values.

- Everyone needs help, and sometimes our stakeholders don't help. Your stakeholders are those who are affected by your behaviors. Our changes can be as uncomfortable for those around us as they are for us. Prepare your friends and family members, and identify those who will support you the most. Also, unhelpful parts of our personalities can be triggered by our new situations. By tapping into Self-energy, we can provide those parts with support. If you'd like additional help, an IFS-informed coach or IFS practitioner can be a great resource. See the Resources for more information.

- It's quite likely that someone else has made the exact same changes you're trying to make. Researching how to change specific traits or the change process in general can provide you with additional knowledge and skills that may support your changes.

- Each tool in your toolbox offers unique advantages, and the support you'll receive from these tools is cumulative. The more tools you use, the more supported you'll feel in your change journey.

As you measure, you have a basis on which to improve.

—ROBIN SHARMA

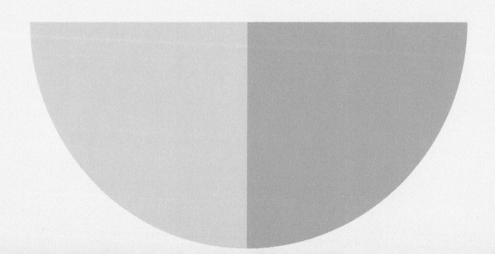

CHAPTER 6

Keeping Track of Your Growth

Without a map, it's difficult to chart your adventure journey toward your goal for success. To tell if you're heading in the right direction, you need to determine your starting point and where you want to end up, and you also need a sense of the time frame for change. If you don't have measurable, observable milestones and benchmarks, you may fall entirely off track without realizing it. If you don't celebrate the small successes, you may become discouraged, lose motivation, and quit.

This chapter will guide you through the process of mapping your change journey in concrete terms, attaching timelines to the smaller steps along the way. As you complete the exercises in this chapter, you'll identify your support network to help you achieve these smaller goals, and you'll create a menu of rewards for celebrating your many wins on the way to your larger goal.

Worse Than Ever

"I need to see you as soon as possible. It's worse than it's ever been," Laura said in her phone message. We'd been working together for several months, and she had made remarkable progress, so much so, in fact, that we had decreased the frequency of her appointments.

Previously, Laura had experienced instances in which irritable behaviors had gotten the better of her. We had worked together on a mindfulness program, and she had taken many of the steps listed in this book. She had taken an honest look at how her behaviors affected friends, family, and coworkers, and she had developed a strong sense of purpose around her change. In addition, she had taken action, using mindfulness-based stress-reduction techniques and several other tools to help her decrease the underlying feelings of irritability.

She had made such great progress! What had happened to set her back? I wondered.

My curiosity piqued, I returned her call.

"You say it's worse than ever. About how many times a day are you currently experiencing irritable behaviors?" I asked.

"Four to seven, at least. I'm so embarrassed I just can't stand it. When can I get in?" she responded.

I reviewed the notes I had taken during our meetings. "Well, I've got some good news and some bad news. The bad news is that the irritable episodes have indeed increased. Last month, you were only experiencing maybe one instance per day," I began. "But the good news is that things aren't actually worse than they were when you started. In fact, they're only half as bad. Initially, you were having about twelve to fifteen instances per day."

As expected, Laura's reaction to this mixed news was . . . also mixed.

THE STORY THE STORY TELLS

Although Laura's problems weren't worse than ever, they were still worse than they had been the month before. What was that about? This became much clearer at our next appointment.

I had kept track of the frequency of Laura's irritable episodes, but she had not, so she had no way to quantify how effectively her plan was working. When things were at their best, Laura rested on her laurels; she didn't establish new contracts with herself to keep moving forward. What's worse, she assumed that because she had done well for a few weeks, she didn't need to worry about this problem anymore.

Perhaps the most important lesson that Laura's story teaches us is that human memory is unreliable. If we don't write things down, we don't remember them as clearly as we imagine we do. Laura thought that her problem behavior was worse than ever, but in fact it was less than half as bad as it had been at the start.

Rather than using her success to fuel additional growth, Laura began second-guessing herself. More than once, she heard that self-critical voice saying that if she were only stronger, she wouldn't need to work this plan in the first place. Her embarrassment about her behavior and her efforts to change it kept her from reaching out to friends or family for support. Plus, she had forgotten about the impact of her behaviors on those around her.

Because memory is imperfect, it's very important that you keep track of your progress. Doing so will give you an accurate sense of where you are in your journey. It's also helpful to have a supportive person in your life who can help you stay on track (a sidekick or accountability buddy). Who will be your sidekick or accountability buddy? And how will you measure your progress?

Record Your Progress to Stay Honest and Motivated

Laura's story demonstrates several important points about navigating this stage of the change journey. One of the most important is the need to monitor your progress in a meaningful way. In other words, find a way to measure your problem before launching your change process, and then perform that measurement frequently to make sure you stay on track.

Because Laura didn't measure her problem behavior to begin with, she had no idea when she could celebrate even small wins. She allowed her self-limiting beliefs to prevent her from reaching out for help in making changes that were important to her. And over time, in the absence of any reminders, she forgot how important those changes were to begin with. As a result, Laura lost motivation.

Think about the thoughts, feelings, and behaviors you're trying to change. How could you measure them? Could you rate troublesome thoughts or feelings on a scale from one to ten every day? Or are your behaviors something you could count? Getting crystal clear on the extent of your problem in a quantifiable way will help you set benchmarks and milestones. You can plan rewards and celebrations for those smaller accomplishments as you continue trekking toward your larger goals.

Laura had no one to keep her honest; she hadn't identified a sidekick or an accountability buddy. Her thinking reverted to earlier patterns. When her problem behaviors initially began to increase, she used rationalization and denial to minimize the problem. Because she didn't have an accountability partner, no one was there to point out the potential problems, remind her of her strengths, and help her focus on her goals.

The truth is, no one achieves anything worthwhile alone. Dorothy, Luke, and Frodo all had sidekicks, and this is true for heroes in the real world, too. Every great leader has had numerous supporters help them. Can you think of a person who would make a great sidekick? Does someone come to mind who will tell you the truth you most need to hear (even when it's difficult), who will lift you when you fall, and who will celebrate your accomplishments with a fully joyful heart?

In this chapter, you'll have an opportunity to keep yourself from duplicating Laura's experience. You'll develop a plan for establishing a measurable end goal. You'll establish some benchmarks and milestones so you can easily identify whether you're on track as you proceed with your plan. You'll create a plan to celebrate each achievement and each action taken, even if you don't see results immediately. You'll also learn how to recruit a sidekick to help you reach your goals.

By using the tools you acquire in this chapter, you'll be able to measure your accomplishments, celebrate your achievements, and keep yourself on track. Let's get started!

1. VISUALIZATION: REVERSE ENGINEERING

Take a comfortable seat somewhere that feels safe and where you know you won't be distracted for a while. Review the end goal you drafted in chapter 4, and imagine having reached that goal one year from now. Take a deep breath, allowing your eyes to close while you hold this vision firmly in your mind.

Now imagine that you can travel backward precisely six months from that time, to six months from now. What have you accomplished by that point in your change process? What evidence do you see, feel, and hear that lets you know you're on track to reach your goals? What still needs work? What do you sense, see, hear, and feel while you're visualizing that lets you know you're not quite there?

Flip the calendar back another three months, to three months from now. What do you observe?

Now turn the calendar back to two months from now. What accomplishments are you proudest of at this point?

Finally, turn the calendar back to thirty days from now. What key changes have you made by that time? What do you sense, see, hear, and/or feel that lets you know you're on track to reach your biggest goal?

Here, you'll transform your visualization in exercise 1 into a set of SMART goals that are relevant to you.

1. Develop a way of measuring the problem behaviors, thoughts, or feelings you're working to change. You can use a scale from zero to ten to identify how severe the problem is, or, even better, if you're working to change a behavior, count how many times the behavior occurs.

2. Describe the problem and your goals so clearly that anyone who reads this chart will know whether or not you succeeded just by observing you for one day.

3. Using what you learned from exercise 1, fill in the chart on page 86 with your current measurement, and establish your thirty-, sixty-, and ninety-day goals.

THOUGHTS

What specific thought patterns, if any, are you working to change? How often do these thoughts arise? How much do they distract you?

_____

_____

_____

_____

_____

_____

FEELINGS

What problematic feelings are you working to overcome? How often do these feelings occur? How severely do they interfere with your feelings of happiness?

_____

_____

_____

_____

_____

_____

BEHAVIORS

What behaviors are you hoping to change? How many times per day or week do these problem behaviors occur?

_____

_____

_____

_____

_____

THIRTY-DAY GOAL	SIXTY-DAY GOAL	NINETY-DAY GOAL
_____	_____	_____
_____	_____	_____
_____	_____	_____
_____	_____	_____
_____	_____	_____
_____	_____	_____
_____	_____	_____
_____	_____	_____
_____	_____	_____
_____	_____	_____
_____	_____	_____
_____	_____	_____
_____	_____	_____
_____	_____	_____
_____	_____	_____
_____	_____	_____

• • • • • • • • • 3. FIND A SIDEKICK • • • • • • • • •

This exercise is a combination of brainstorming and concrete planning around finding a sidekick. If you don't have a sidekick, visit the resources section for suggestions of groups where you might meet one.

Brainstorming: Generate a few names for each question.

1. Who might exercise or practice mindfulness-based stress reduction

   with me? _____

2. Whom can I count on to be my cheerleaders? _____

3. Who can help me make changes to my environment (for example, remove

   temptation, reduce stressors)? _____

Planning: Select your sidekicks and set a timeline to ask them for help.

I will invite _____ to be my change partner by this

date: _____. I will ask _____ to exercise

with me _____ times per week by this date: _____.

I am comfortable asking these people to be my cheerleaders:

_____ and _____. I will ask them to support

my change plan by doing the following things: _____,

_____, _____, and _____.

These are the changes I need to make in my environment to support

my growth: _____, _____, _____.

Within the next _____ days, I will ask _____

and _____ for help making those changes.

SELF-LIMITING BELIEFS

Act 2 of your new story of you brings a unique cluster of self-limiting beliefs to the surface for many people. Let's take a look.

Avoidance leads us to think, "I can do this on my own; I don't need a sidekick." Behind those thoughts is the belief that asking for help signals weakness. Even if you just moved to a new city or have lost your support system for other reasons, it's possible to create a new support system. A great way to start would be to reach out to a support group like one of the ones listed in the resources section at the back of this book.

What reminders can you set on your phone to counter those thoughts? Set them now.

Thoughts such as "That problem wasn't so bad," "It doesn't matter if I change or not," and "I wasn't hurting anybody but myself" are characteristic of denial. Beneath those thoughts are parts that are invested in maintaining our problems; they found comfort in your old patterns, and they're very uncomfortable with change.

One technique I find useful for soothing the parts that are distressed by change is to remind myself of this: "I bring supportive Self-energy to struggling parts." Try saying it yourself. Then take a moment to practice a mindfulness technique to soothe that part. Reminding yourself of the ways that your behaviors were harming you will also help you break through denial.

If you find yourself thinking, "I don't need to change my environment" or "I don't need to monitor my progress, I'm doing fine," you might be experiencing overconfidence. These thought patterns work alongside other self-limiting beliefs to undermine our ability to manage environmental triggers, which can lead to problematic thoughts, feelings, and behaviors. Remembering that no environment is completely temptation-free will help you stay dedicated to making the environmental changes that are possible. Progressively increasing your stress tolerance will help you navigate situations that are beyond your control.

•••••••••• 4. HORIZON CONTRACTS ••••••••••

A horizon contract is a short-term contract that you make with yourself or one of your sidekicks. It breaks your larger goals into smaller steps.

Imagine that the treasure you seek on this growth journey is on the other side of a mountain, out of sight. The bend in the trail on the ridge up ahead is the farthest point you can see, and you estimate that it will take an hour to get there. Your horizon contract is to reach that ridge within an hour. As you hike, your horizon changes, and you make new horizon contracts as you go along. When you reach the summit, you can see your destination, which is about a two-day hike from the summit. This is the final horizon contract for this goal.

Let's say Frank wants to better manage his anger. His first horizon contract is, for one week, to leave heated situations without losing his temper and take a five-minute meditation instead. After a successful week, his next horizon contract is to do the same for one month. After several months, his new horizon contract is his final goal: to stay in the room and remain calm during difficult conversations.

Write your first horizon contract on the following lines. Share it with one of your sidekicks.

_____

_____

_____

_____

_____

_____

5. RECORDING PROGRESS

You now have your one-week contract established, and your thirty-, sixty-, and ninety-day goals written in a way that aligns with your end point and keeps you on the timeline you're hoping for. Now it's time to decide how you'll record your progress.

1. Conduct your own research and reflect on your own habits to determine which method is likely to be the best fit for you.

2. Implement your selected method today by recording your baseline information.

   - Read through the following options.

   - Create a timeline that you can post visibly in your home.

   - Fill in a spreadsheet using Excel, Numbers, or a similar program.

   - Keep an activity log or journal, such as the *Your Personality and You Journal.*

   - Record your progress on a whiteboard or blank paper placed on the wall.

   - Set calendar events for thirty-, sixty-, and ninety-day check-ins. Record your progress on your calendar.

   - Use an app or online service such as Habit Tracker or Daytum.

• • • • • • 6. CELEBRATING SUCCESSES • • • • • •

One key to staying motivated is having a willingness to celebrate successes. Create a mix of short- and long-term (or cumulative) rewards. It's important to celebrate actions taken, even if the results aren't exactly what you were hoping for.

For example, I'm working to replace the unhealthy habits I've picked up recently, and I also want to get back into the habit of regular exercise. I'm paying myself $2 for every mile I bike. I get the money, which I'll spend on a new bike, even if I don't lose any weight. That's my long-term reward. In the short term, I reward myself with an episode of my favorite TV show for each outing on my bike.

The following are other ideas to consider:

- A bubble bath

- An hour of video games

- An indulgent coffee drink

- Lunch with a friend

- A new accessory or article of clothing OR a new book, notebook, or other small item

- Ordering out dinner

- A walk or hike

For a cumulative goal, consider saving money for one of the following:

- Equipment for a hobby (golf clubs, weights or exercise equipment, professional artist-quality paints and canvases, etc.)

- A new bicycle

- A new car

- A vacation

What rewards might inspire you to keep moving forward?

Key Takeaways

- Our memory does not always serve us correctly. Study after study has shown that even people who don't have any memory impairment still remember details incorrectly. The mind is more like a piece of impressionist art than a high-definition photograph, partly because what we recall is often shaped by emotions felt both at the time of the event and afterward. For that reason, it's very important that you keep track of your progress. Accurately keeping track of your progress will help you stay motivated.

- How do you eat an elephant? One bite at a time. Similarly, you'll tackle your larger change goals by setting goals for shorter periods. Setting one-week and thirty-, sixty-, and ninety-day goals will keep your focus sharp and prevent you from getting overwhelmed. Of course, you may have to adjust those goals based on unforeseen circumstances. But once you chart the journey, you'll always know where you stand in relation to that goal.

- Celebrate every success—every single one. Celebrating actions taken is important, especially when it may take some time to reach your longer-term goals. Create a menu of potential rewards that will motivate you to keep taking one step forward.

- Maintain your mindset. Certain self-limiting beliefs are common during this stage of the change process. By being aware of avoidance, denial, and overconfidence, you can avoid some of the common pitfalls they lead to. The tools you learned about in this chapter can help you counteract all three.

The point is, everything operates as a system ... [and] systems resist change.

—JAMES D. MURPHY

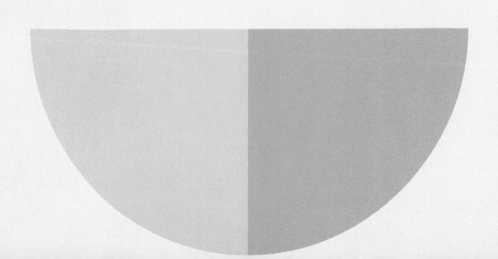

CHAPTER 7

Tackling Obstacles and Embracing Failure

In many superhero stories, a passage will often arise in which it appears the hero will fail. When we're reading adventure stories, these challenges and setbacks add drama and keep us interested. They force the hero to develop or display a new quality or strength that will bring the story to a resolution. Those challenges, obstacles, and failures make an adventure story what it is.

In our own story of change, setbacks can have the opposite effect. Most often, people who experience setbacks or failures during their change process try to overcome their obstacles by taking the very approaches that didn't work before. Some people become filled with self-doubt and shame and then give up entirely.

Successful self-changers use obstacles, setbacks, and failures as opportunities to develop new self-awareness and skills that will help them achieve their goals. The exercises in this chapter will help you do the same.

Turning Obstacles to Stepping Stones

"I know he's not marriage material. But I'm going through a lot right now, and I just don't have what it takes to wait for something better to come around," Lydia said to the group. Lydia was in her mid-forties and divorced, and she was raising two teenagers while working full time. She had come to a Mindful Dating Coaching Group to learn new relationship skills so she could create a lasting, healthy relationship. But when her seventy-three-year-old mother suffered a stroke and needed full-time care, Lydia fell into her old relationship patterns. She dove into a deep relationship with someone she knew was wrong for her because she needed comfort and security.

Carmen, another group member, was also having a difficult time changing her relationship patterns. She struggled with commitment and tended to be attracted to partners who were emotionally unavailable. Her biggest challenge was in completing the homework exercises. "I just don't see how visualizations, meditation, and affirmations are going to help me on dates. What I need are tips on how to meet people," she said repeatedly.

"This is too much work. If it's meant to be, it will be," Renata said. Prone to short-term and disappointing relationships, Renata had joined the group primarily because she was a friend of Lydia's and thought it would be something fun to do together. She was unprepared for the amount of work it would take to make lasting change in her relationship style.

Rachel, on the other hand, was in a stress-free period in her life. She understood that having a healthy relationship would require her to learn and practice many skills, and she was fully prepared to do the work. But she was still struggling. "My friends think this is all weird. This just isn't the approach they're taking to relationships. I feel so alone," she said.

THE STORY THE STORY TELLS

Slipups are normal during the change process, and they can happen at any time. The stories of the women in the Mindful Dating Coaching Group reveal the most common reasons for setbacks.

Sometimes life is overwhelming, causing people to slip back into old patterns that were often originally developed out of a misplaced desire for comfort. If stress-management skills and resources aren't firmly in place, life stressors can push you off course. That was Lydia's experience.

Carmen slipped up because she didn't realize that personal growth requires using many methods simultaneously. Willpower alone is never enough to carry you safely and happily through the change process. This book has introduced you to many tools, and the hope is that you've been willing to step outside your comfort zone and try all of them.

Renata hadn't set her change goal with a purpose. She wasn't clear on the potential benefits of a stable, loving relationship or the potential cost of not having one. If you don't have clarity around how you'll benefit from making the changes you're considering, you're more likely to give up. Be sure that you're wise to your whys.

Like many people who make big changes, Rachel discovered that her social circle was uncomfortable with her new way of behaving. This can occur with family and work relationships as well as friendships. For some people, the threat of losing these close relationships overwhelms their desire for change. This, too, can result in a slipup.

Stumbling is an inevitable part of the change process. But if you're prepared for act 2 of your new story of you, challenges, obstacles, and setbacks can become a part of the story rather than the end of the world (or your efforts). Setbacks and obstacles can be your greatest teachers—if you're willing to learn from them.

Don't Let Setbacks Make You Step Back

Why are setbacks so common in the change process? As the opening quotation for the chapter suggests, all changes occur within systems, and all systems resist change. Each of us has our own inner system within our hearts and minds. Very often, the problems we're working on were, at an earlier time, solutions for a different problem. Your inner system will be inclined to resist changing any processes that it perceives as useful.

Behaviors that signal inner-system resistance include a reliance on willpower, an unwillingness to learn or practice new skills, and a refusal to research the cost of our problem behaviors. Pause to reflect on how you have felt as you've encountered the exercises in this book. Are you putting your best foot forward with each one, or are you skipping many of them because they invite you to try things that are outside your comfort zone?

If you observe some of these behaviors in yourself, you'll find this chapter especially helpful. Several exercises will help you identify and address this resistance. In addition, if you feel that your inner system is resisting the changes you're making, consider visiting exercise 2 from chapter 5. That exercise will help you get all those mixed emotions out on paper so you can understand how they relate to one another. Then you can bring Self-energy to your struggling parts.

We also exist within external systems: friendship circles, family structures, work environments. These systems also resist change. Our growth may be perceived as threatening, even to people who love us dearly. Our personal changes cause inevitable shifts in those systems. Reassuring loved ones that you're committed to them can help allay their fears. In some cases, people need to shift their social circles to remain on track and create lasting change. Building your support network and focusing on your goal can be helpful in maintaining your growth orientation in the face of those challenges.

Sometimes, despite our best efforts, life happens. We find ourselves in a situation beyond our control. Loved ones die, cars collide, bosses get demanding, and people get sick. Any person on earth could face a situation in which stress exceeds their coping capacity. The key in situations like these is to accept that you're a human being and recommit to your growth process.

The exercises in this chapter were designed to help you learn from any setbacks that may occur. You'll learn a powerful meditation for managing stress. Several of the exercises will demonstrate an effective process for learning from setbacks so you can continue writing your new story of you. After all, every adventure story has a point in the middle where it looks like all hope is lost. The key to resolution is to learn the lessons that the setback teaches and to keep moving toward your goals.

• • • • • 1. MINDFULNESS EXERCISE: • • • • • TREE OF LIFE MEDITATION

This mindfulness exercise is a wonderful way to release any overwhelming emotions.

1. Stand with your feet together, your arms at your sides, and your palms facing forward.

2. Inhale deeply and imagine the energy of life flowing from the crown of your head downward through the bottoms of your feet.

3. Feel the solidity of the ground beneath your feet. Allow it to fill you with confidence and courage.

4. As you breathe, imagine yourself in the shape of a tree, with your body as the trunk and energetic roots that extend deep into the earth. As you inhale, imagine any excess nervous energies flowing down through your legs and feet, getting carried deep within the earth below by your roots.

5. As you exhale, imagine pushing the nervous energies even more deeply into the earth, which takes in any overwhelming emotions. The earth absorbs millions of lightning strikes every day and keeps spinning, and it can also absorb your anxiety and excess energies.

6. With your next inhalation, imagine drawing nourishment upward through the energetic roots, through the bottoms of your feet, and up through your spine. Allow the calm, nurturing energy of the earth to fill your body completely, then breathe out any extra nurturing calm into the world around you.

• • • • • • • • • • 2. WHAT HAPPENED? • • • • • • • • • •

The difference between a setback and complete failure is determined by whether you get back on track with your changes or give up. It doesn't do much good to try again if you simply repeat the same flawed plans. This exercise will help you learn from your setbacks so you can get back on track to success.

1. Get out a sheet of paper and turn it sideways.

2. Draw a line from left to right.

3. On the far right, identify how you slipped. Mark the events and circumstances in your life that led to the event. Sometimes a setback can occur in stages. For example, someone trying to lose weight might have two cookies every day for a week and then binge on the eighth day.

4. See if you can identify any of these minor slipups, then add them to your timeline.

• • • • • • • • • • 3. WHAT DID I MISS? • • • • • • • • • •

When people experience setbacks in their change process, it's quite often the result of having missed an earlier step (Prochaska et al., 1995). The exercises you've completed thus far in this book are grounded in the theory of change and reflect the steps in the change process. If you've experienced a setback, it's important to review the steps you've taken to see if you gave an exercise inadequate attention or even missed something entirely.

- Review the exercises you've completed so far.

- Which exercises did you skip entirely?

- Which exercises could you have given greater attention?

- How might revisiting the exercises help you overcome your current setback?

- Which exercises are you finding yourself doing consistently and well?

- How can you celebrate your commitment to those parts of the change process that you're doing well and with enthusiasm?

SELF-LIMITING BELIEFS

Setbacks, slipups, and obstacles are very common, so much so that they're considered a normal part of the change process. As we discussed in chapter 1, people with a growth mindset are more likely to rebound from setbacks. That's because a fixed mindset leaves people vulnerable to particular self-limiting beliefs. Let's take a look at self-limiting beliefs common to this stage of change and create antidotes together.

"I am incapable of change."

Someone with this self-limiting belief views setbacks and failures as an indicator of their lack of the innate ability to achieve their goals. They overlook what they have managed to accomplish and instead focus on the setback.

"I need to try harder."

Because people with a fixed mindset believe that talent is something people are born with, they tend to rely on the same tools repeatedly. Instead of recognizing that their setbacks indicate a need to learn new tools, they double down on the tools they already have.

"I have to do it by myself."

For people with a fixed mindset, asking for help can be viewed as a failure all by itself. "After all," they think, "if I had to ask for help, that means that I'm not capable of doing this."

The growth process requires a commitment to ongoing growth and development. If you're struggling with a fixed mindset, or any self-limiting beliefs, see if some of these modifications might be effective antidotes:

- "The power to change my life is in my hands."

- "I have learned many things, and I can learn how to overcome this obstacle."

- "Failure is a sign that it's time to try some new tools."

• • • • • • • 4. MEETING RESISTANCE • • • • • • •

Review the timeline you constructed. What inner-system resistance, outer-system resistance, or circumstances may have contributed to your setback?

Inner-system resistance:

☐ I became overconfident and quit using the tools that were working.

☐ I didn't connect my change to a sense of purpose.

☐ I haven't been using the tools provided in this book on a regular basis.

☐ I let self-limiting beliefs sidetrack me.

☐ I was afraid to set boundaries with others.

☐ Other: _____

Outer-system resistance:

☐ Criticism, pushback, or ridicule from friends, family, or significant others

☐ Friends, family, or coworkers unwilling to help me change my environment

☐ A lot of temptations or stressors in my neighborhood that I can't change

☐ Other: _____

Circumstances:

- ☐ Car accident
- ☐ Damage to home or loss of housing
- ☐ Death of loved one
- ☐ Divorce or breakup
- ☐ Illness of self or loved one
- ☐ Job loss
- ☐ Natural disaster
- ☐ New child
- ☐ Recent move
- ☐ Other: _____

• • • • • • 5. WHAT CAN I DO ABOUT IT? • • • • • •

Reflect on the following questions, then answer in the spaces provided.

What would it take for you to overcome your inner-system resistance and feel completely invested in your own success?

_____

_____

_____

_____

Which exercises would you like to repeat (or do for the first time if you skipped them)?

_____

_____

_____

_____

What can you do to overcome system resistance?

_____

_____

_____

_____

What support do you need to navigate external circumstances that are causing you to slip up?

_____

_____

_____

_____

What priorities might need to shift to support your change process?

_____

_____

_____

_____

What is one step you can take today to affirm your commitment to your new story of you?

_____

_____

_____

_____

• • • • • • • • 6. WHO CAN HELP ME? • • • • • • • •

Sometimes, no matter how hard you try, you can't make changes happen on your own, even with a helpful book such as this one. Answer the following yes-or-no prompts to get a sense of whether to seek additional help and what to look for.

1. I feel like I'm the only person struggling with this problem.   **Y   N**
   If you answered yes, you may benefit from a support group.

2. I've tried to change many times, and nothing works.   **Y   N**

3. I don't have supportive relationships in my life.   **Y   N**

4. No matter how hard I try, I can't understand how to make change happen.   **Y   N**

   If you answered yes to questions 2, 3, or 4, you might benefit from the services of a life coach.

5. Symptoms of a major mental health disorder interfere with my change process.   **Y   N**

6. I'm experiencing difficulties functioning, such as loss of appetite, poor sleep, or inability to concentrate.   **Y   N**

   If you answered yes to questions 5 or 6, you may benefit from the help of a licensed mental health provider.

See the Resources section for help finding a support group, life coach, or mental health professional.

Key Takeaways

- Unlike adventure stories, personal change does not have a beginning, a middle, and an end. Instead, change is more like a spiral. Very often, people experience setbacks that force them to revisit earlier stages, but they're not in the same exact place when they go back there. They bring new insights and experiences that help them circulate through the stages more quickly.

- Failure is a great teacher—if you're willing to learn from it. That doesn't mean you should rush out and fail. Instead, it means that if you're willing to analyze the factors that contributed to your setback and take action to adjust your approach, you'll learn a lot about change in general and yourself in particular.

- The devil is in the details: Reviewing the events and circumstances leading to your setback or failure in detail will provide you with a lot of information about how and why it occurred. The results of your analysis can be used to formulate an action plan to get yourself back on track.

- Help is available: You don't have to learn alone. No matter what you're trying to change, chances are good that you're not the first to try. If you're struggling with overwhelming life circumstances, repeated failures, or an inadequate support system, reaching out for more formal help is something to strongly consider. See the Resources section for referral sources.

Yes, I am imperfect and vulnerable and sometimes afraid, but that doesn't change the truth that I am also brave and worthy of love and belonging.

—BRENÉ BROWN

CHAPTER 8

Practicing Self-Love

At last, we arrive at act 3, the resolution stage, in which the hero achieves the goal. But even as the story draws to a close, we intuitively know that the new harmony is incomplete or will be difficult to maintain. Sometimes we even think to ourselves, "I bet they're making a sequel."

The resolution of your new story of you requires that you integrate self-love into your practices. Many exercises throughout this book no doubt have helped you with this already, but now this practice will become clearer for what it is: a way of developing your inner resources so that you can continue personal growth as a lifelong adventure.

Many people fear that practicing self-love will make them more self-ish. This chapter clarifies the ways in which self-love is a practice that, instead, gives you more to share with the world. The exercises in this chapter will help you identify the many people who will benefit from your commitment to self-love.

Never Enough

"I've got to get this under control. My doctor says my blood sugar and cholesterol levels are in the danger zone. My wife says I'm emotionally unavailable, whatever that means. And I'm not getting results at work," Dan said.

Dan sought coaching for help achieving a higher level of performance in his role as executive director of a small social services organization. His work was important not only to him, but also to the hundreds of people his agency served, not to mention the employees working under his leadership. Public health emergencies brought about a dramatic increase in folks needing help and, unfortunately, a parallel decrease in donations. He wanted to elevate his performance so he could navigate his organization through rough waters.

"At first, I really loved working from home. I could hold Zoom meetings early in the morning before the kids were up, and I could write reports after they went to bed," Dan explained. Initially, working from home was a godsend. Throughout the waxing and waning impact of this change in routine on his work and family life, Dan's response was to give even more.

Over time, Dan slipped into a bedtime routine of snacking on chips and cookies while binge-watching TV series online. He'd put on quite a bit of weight. As a result, he'd become very self-critical of his appearance and lack of self-control. None of that stopped his bingeing habits, however.

But self-criticism alone was not enough to motivate Dan. Instead, self-criticism led him to overextend himself to meet his own unrealistic demands. Continued failure to meet his unreasonable standards caused his feelings of failure and inadequacy to become overwhelming. At that point, Dan's system decided that the best course of action was to withdraw and seek comfort in familiar TV shows and a variety of snacks.

THE STORY THE STORY TELLS

"I know things are tough for everyone, and I get that I'm spread pretty thin, but there's a part of me that thinks I should be handling everything so much better than I am," Dan said in one of his early coaching sessions.

Dan was driven by the best of intentions to serve his community in a time of need. In the process, he'd become a demanding taskmaster. And to make matters worse, his inability to reach his own unrealistic goals brought a self-critical part of himself to the surface.

Dan's ability to see that the self-critical part was just that—a *part*—opened a pathway for us to use an IFS-informed approach to helping him develop greater access to Self-energy and experience greater self-love as a result. Chapter 1 introduced the IFS model of "the 8 C's of Self": calmness, clarity, compassion, confidence, connection, courage, creativity, and curiosity. This model affirms that these qualities are the authentic core of every human being.

With time, Dan became better able to access Self-energy, to cope with stress, and to be more compassionate about his remaining imperfections. He also experienced *less* stress because he wasn't adding the burden of self-criticism to an already challenging situation. As a result, he no longer reached the point of being so overwhelmed that he would shut down.

"It turns out the airlines are right: You have to put your own oxygen mask on first, or you won't be able to help anyone else," Dan said several weeks into coaching. "I didn't realize how much *my* stress was affecting everyone around me."

Once Dan began practicing self-love, he became more compassionate and loving with his family, friends, and coworkers. He recognized that even if he couldn't solve the problems the COVID-19 pandemic brought to everyone's life, he could support them better by caring for himself.

Love Is a Greater Motivator Than Shame

Many people become self-critical when they begin thinking about ways to practice self-love. They confuse self-love with self-indulgence. Just as a loving parent won't allow a child to eat only chocolate cake every day, you won't indulge your less-than-ideal impulses when you love yourself fully.

If fear, shame, or guilt were your motivating forces, you would face an uphill battle in your change journey. Those emotions add to the burdens of negative self-talk and stress that you'd have to contend with along the way. Those emotions also lead us to fixed-mindset thinking. Negative self-talk would make it more difficult for you to overcome the inevitable setbacks you'll face in your life. You'll also likely find it harder to ask for support when you need it. And why would you invest the energy needed to change when you don't feel you're worth it?

When you allow genuine, nurturing self-love to motivate your change process, you'll have more resources to devote to self-improvement. Self-love is similar to having a loving parent. When you love yourself fully, you'll nourish your mind, body, and soul. You'll be patient with your growth process, too. You'll celebrate progress instead of demanding perfection. You'll love yourself unconditionally, even if you don't like absolutely everything about yourself. As a result, your growth process will become infused with love rather than shame and guilt. When you love yourself unconditionally, you'll be steadfast in asking for the help you need.

In short, self-love is a more effective motivator of positive change than shame or guilt. With the guidance of self-love, you'll have more motivation to invest yourself fully in your well-being, doing whatever it takes to see the project through to the end. Not only that, but it turns out that practicing self-love does not just benefit yourself; it is also an act of service to others.

At the start of every commercial flight, the flight attendants advise passengers that if they are traveling with a small child and the oxygen masks drop down, they should put on their own oxygen mask first and then help the child. This can be a metaphor for why self-love is so important: If we sacrifice ourselves, we have nothing left to give others.

Each of us exists within a network of family, friends, coworkers, and community. We not only receive benefits from this network, but we also contribute to the well-being of all those around us. If we're not at our best, we can't give our best to others. Our bad moods affect the people with whom we live and work. When we're unwell, other people have to work harder to pick up the slack.

Each of us affects many other people. It's important that we practice self-love so that we have the best possible impact. Self-love provides the emotional resources you need to become the best possible version of yourself. You can only give others what you have, so if you fill yourself with self-love, compassion, and unconditional acceptance, you'll be able to offer those attributes to others as well.

• • • • • • 1. MINDFULNESS PRACTICE: • • • • • •
LOVING-KINDNESS MEDITATION

Studies have shown that compassion-based mindfulness practices such as this one help people not only develop self-compassion, but also become more compassionate toward others.

1. Sit comfortably with your eyes closed, one hand over your heart and one hand over your belly. Take a deep breath and imagine moving the powerful energy of loving-kindness downward through the top of your head to your belly. Say to yourself, "May I be filled with loving-kindness."

2. As you exhale, imagine the energy flowing outward from your belly in a graceful arc, turning back toward your heart. The energy fills your heart completely before it flows outward through the back of your heart in an arc behind you on its way back to your belly.

3. As you breathe, the energy continues to circulate, building with each pass.

4. As the warmth and light build, imagine them flowing outward like ripples in a pond. The first ripple moves through a circle of your closest friends and family. Say to them, "May you be filled with loving-kindness." The energy continues rippling outward, through other circles of connection: friends, coworkers, neighbors, acquaintances, and, finally, your community. Say to yourself, "May they be filled with loving-kindness."

5. Breathe in the loving-kindness you're generating. Bow in gratitude for your ability to generate loving-kindness, release that energy freely outward, and open your eyes.

Draw a nesting set of circles in the space that follows, one inside the other like a bull's-eye. These are the ripples in your pond. First, specify who is in the first ripple: your closest friends and family. Then, identify who is in the next ripple: the people you interact with regularly, even if you're not emotionally close. Last, note those who are in the distant ripples: those you interact with infrequently. Write all their names in the appropriate circles. How can you affect each ripple more positively by practicing self-love?

• • • • • • • 3. CREATIVE EXPRESSION • • • • • • •

Creative expression connects us with core Self-energy. Select a creative activity from the following list, or select one of your own. Prepare for the activity if needed, and set aside thirty to sixty minutes for creative expression.

☐ Dancing: at home, alone, to whatever music lights you up inside

☐ Drawing: abstract drawings, landscapes, still lifes

☐ Creating found art: going for a nature walk and collecting items you find along the way; arranging them into a mini art piece

☐ Painting: with kids' or professional artists' paints

☐ Pottery: signing up for a pottery class at your local park district or community college, or purchasing oven-bake polymer clay from a craft store

☐ Singing: uplifting songs or those you just make up

☐ Writing: short stories, memoirs, poetry

☐ Other: _____

What changes do you notice after you're done with your creative activity? How do you feel emotionally? How do you feel physically?

_____

SELF-LIMITING BELIEFS

Self-love can be one of the most challenging practices of the entire change journey. Most people who launch themselves into change do so because they see something about themselves or their lives that they believe needs to be fixed. Because so much attention can be focused on what's wrong with a person, it's hard to see what there is to love, and people hold many common misconceptions about self-love.

"I'll be worthy of self-love when I _____."

Many people believe they can't devote time and attention to self-care (the most basic practice of self-love) until everything else is done. They believe they have to achieve their goals *first*, and then they'll be loveable. The problem is that because they don't learn to love themselves, they're always seeing flaws to fix. Focusing on self-improvement eventually wears thin, and they become discouraged because they believe they're not good enough.

"Self-love means I'm selfish."

Many people believe that self-love comes at the expense of loving others. They think it means they have to put themselves first all the time, before those they love. They could instead begin to see that self-love replenishes emotional resources, giving them more to offer to those they love. In other words, self-love provides us with more to give to others.

Fear of appearing judgmental.

Sometimes our intention to change for the better means that we have to change our friendship circle. We need to spend time with others who are capable of supporting our changes and who share our commitment to growth. When those decisions need to happen, some people might feel as if they're being judgmental toward former friends. Alternatively, they could choose to admire the way they're taking a stand on behalf of their own well-being.

• • • • • • • • • • • 4. WHEEL OF LIFE • • • • • • • • • • •

Draw a large circle in the space on this page. This circle represents your current life. Divide the circle into eight wedges. Each wedge represents a dimension of wellness: emotional, environmental, financial, intellectual, physical, professional, social, and spiritual. Label each wedge.

Rate your wellness in each of the eight dimensions, on a scale from one to ten, using the pie chart you create. If you like, you can color in each pie piece corresponding to its numeric rating.

Reflect on your Wheel of Life:

- Is your wheel balanced?

- If not, what would it take for you to achieve greater balance?

- Which areas, if any, did you rate as six or lower?

- What would it take for you to boost that number to nine?

_____

_____

_____

_____

_____

_____

_____

_____

_____

_____

_____

_____

• • • • • • • • • 5. PAY IT FORWARD • • • • • • • • •

For some people, committing to paying it forward helps them address the part of them that sees self-love as selfish. One of the benefits of cultivating self-love is that you have more loving-kindness to share with others. There are many small ways you can spread loving-kindness generously. Which of the following appeal to you? Choose a different one each week, and add your own to the list.

- Bring cookies or other treats to a neighbor.

- Do one chore or favor for someone else in your household each week.

- Greet every person you meet with a smile when you are out exercising or running errands.

- Pick up trash while walking in your neighborhood or local park.

- Post an inspirational meme or quotation on social media daily.

- Put snack bars in your car to give to people on the street who might be hungry.

- Send a birthday text, email, or social media greeting to one of your contacts every day.

- Share one wellness practice with a close friend or family member each week.

- Volunteer in a school or community center.

- While making eye contact, tell someone close to you why they're so lovable to you.

- Write a card or letter expressing your gratitude for a different person in your life each week.

- _____

- _____

- _____

•••••• 6. PLANNING THE SEQUEL ••••••

Congratulations! You've arrived at the final exercise of this book. As is so often the case with adventure stories, every ending is a sequel in the making. Take a moment to reflect on your accomplishments as you move forward into your own next adventure.

What have you accomplished in this change process that you're proudest of?

_____

_____

_____

_____

If you could give your former self one piece of advice, what would it be?

_____

_____

_____

_____

How would you revise your change contract to include your newfound emphasis on self-love?

_____

_____

_____

_____

_____

Now that you've had the opportunity to amaze yourself, what is the next challenge you'd like to tackle?

_____

_____

_____

_____

_____

Key Takeaways

- Self-love is an act of service. You serve your own highest good when you love yourself unconditionally, right this very moment. You are worthy of love this moment, even with all your imperfections. When you love yourself in this way, you tap into even greater resources to share with others in your life.

- Wellness practices constitute a vital practice of self-love. Wellness is multifaceted, so your wellness plan should be multifaceted, too. Each dimension of wellness becomes a resource or strength for developing the others. For example, chapter 5 notes that physical wellness (that is, physical exercise) supports emotional wellness by reducing stress and regulating mood.

- A commitment to paying it forward may help build resistance to the self-limiting beliefs described in this chapter. By committing to sharing your self-love with others, you are immediately disproving the negative thinking that tends to see self-love as selfish.

- Finally, self-love will help you embrace personal growth as a lifelong process. You'll never be perfect, but the good news is that you don't have to be. You are worthy of love now, and a commitment to lifelong growth is a demonstration of that love, as is the commitment to continually becoming an even better version of yourself.

*To love oneself is the beginning of
a life-long romance.*

—OSCAR WILDE

RESOURCES

Online Resources

American Psychiatric Association
finder.psychiatry.org
A directory of psychiatrists from the American Association of Psychiatrists.

IFS Institute
ifs-institute.com/practitioners
A provider of IFS training for professionals and a directory for those looking for IFS-trained practitioners.

International Coaching Federation
coachingfederation.org/find-a-coach
Nonprofit accrediting body for coaches; offers a directory of accredited coaches.

Mental Health America
mhanational.org/find-support-groups
A community-based nonprofit dedicated to promoting the overall mental health of all; offers a directory of support groups.

Northwestern University
northwestern.edu/wellness/8-dimensions
There are numerous opinions on the number of dimensions of wellness. This book adopts the perspective of this Northwestern University resource.

***Psychology Today*'s Find a Therapist**
psychologytoday.com/us/therapists
An online referral network operated by *Psychology Today*.

Substance Abuse and Mental Health Services Administration National Helpline
samhsa.gov/find-help/national-helpline
A treatment referral and information website operated by the government agency responsible for advancing the behavioral health of Americans.

Books

Dweck, Carol S. *Mindset: The New Psychology of Success*. New York: Ballantine Books, 2008.
Success in nearly every endeavor is influenced by how we think, particularly whether we have a fixed mindset or a growth mindset.

Neff, Kristin. *Self-Compassion: The Proven Power of Being Kind to Yourself*. London: Hodder & Stoughton, 2013.
Dr. Neff is a leading expert on self-compassion. In this book, she explains how to use self-compassion to heal destructive patterns.

Prochaska, James O., John C. Norcross, and Carlo C. DiClemente. *Changing for Good: A Revolutionary Six-Stage Program for Overcoming Bad Habits and Moving Your Life Positively Forward*. New York: HarpersCollins, 1995.
This groundbreaking book offers simple self-assessments and concrete examples of how people change their own behaviors.

Rezac, Matthew. *Mindfulness Activities for Adults: 50 Simple Exercises to Relax, Stay Present, and Find Peace*. Emeryville, CA: Rockridge Press, 2021.
Stress management is essential on a change journey, and this book has many exercises to help you do just that.

Rosenberg, Marshall B. *Nonviolent Communication: A Language of Compassion*. Del Mar, CA: PuddleDancer Press, 2002.
Compassionate communication is, first and foremost, an excellent tool for self-discovery. It will also help you communicate more effectively.

Schwartz, Richard C. *No Bad Parts: Healing Trauma and Restoring Wholeness with the Internal Family Systems Model*. Boulder, CO: Sounds True, 2021
A clear and concise overview of the Internal Family Systems model; it also provides exercises to help you access Self-energy and work with parts.

Videos

Brewer, Judson. "A Simple Way to Break a Bad Habit." Filmed November 2015, TED video, 9:15. ted.com/talks/judson_brewer_a_simple_way_to _break_a_bad_habit.
Support for stopping the behaviors you find troublesome.

Brown, Brené. "The Power of Vulnerability." Filmed June 2010, TED video, 20:03. ted.com/talks/brene_brown_the_power_of_vulnerability.
A wonderful explanation of how accepting our limitations and vulnerabilities enhances relationships.

Dweck, Carol. "The Power of Believing That You Can Improve." Filmed November 2014. TED video, 10:11. ted.com/talks/carol_dweck_the_power _of_believing_that_you_can_improve.
An excellent summary of the distinction between growth mindset and fixed mindset.

Neff, Kristin. "Why Self-Compassion Is Important." 17:05. youtube.com /watch?v=N6zZb_MM6Jw.
How developing self-compassion is key to navigating the ups and downs of the change process.

Rosenberg, Marshall. "The Basics of Non Violent Communication 1.1." 9:00. youtube.com/watch?v=M-129JLTjkQ.
Learning nonviolent communication will help with assertiveness and anger management, and it will make you a stronger leader.

Steindle-Rast, David. "Want to Be Happy? Be Grateful." Filmed June 2013. TED video, 14:17. ted.com/talks/david_steindl_rast_want_to_be_happy _be_grateful.
Practicing gratitude will improve your mood and help you navigate change by focusing on the positive.

Apps

Calm
calm.com
App that provides help with anxiety, focus, and sleep.

Insight Timer
insighttimer.com
App that provides numerous meditations and mindfulness trainings conducted by a variety of teachers to help people manage stress and anxiety and sleep better.

MapMyRun
mapmyrun.com
App that tracks your runs, hikes, and bike rides.

Noom
noom.com
App that helps with weight loss and stress management.

REFERENCES

Brown, Brené. *The Gifts of Imperfection: 10th Anniversary Edition*. New York: Random House, 2020.

_____. *Rising Strong: How the Ability to Reset Transforms the Way We Live, Love, Parent, and Lead*. New York: Random House, 2017.

Capra, Fritjof. *The Web of Life: A New Scientific Understanding of Living Systems*. New York: Anchor Books, 1997.

Cooper, Stewart E. "Systematic Eclecticism: A Pragmatic Approach to Integrating Counseling Methods." *The School Counselor* 35, no. 2 (November 1987): 96–101. jstor.org/stable/23903430.

Courson, Ben. *Optimisfits: Igniting a Fierce Rebellion against Hopelessness*. Eugene, OR: Harvest House Publishers, 2019.

Dweck, Carol S. *Mindset: The New Psychology of Success*. New York: Ballantine Books, 2008.

Epstein, Mark. *Going to Pieces without Falling Apart: A Buddhist Perspective on Wholeness*. New York: Broadway Books, 1998.

Gilbert, Elizabeth. *Big Magic: Creative Living beyond Fear*. New York: Riverhead Books, 2015.

Goleman, Daniel, and Richard J. Davidson. *Altered Traits: Science Reveals How Meditation Changes Your Mind, Brain, and Body*. New York: Avery, 2018

Hafiz. *The Gift: Poems by Hafiz, the Great Sufi Master*. Translated by Daniel Ladinsky. New York: Arkana, 1999.

Harvard Business Review, Daniel Goleman, Richard Boyatzis, Annie McKee, and Sydney Finkelstein. *HBR's 10 Must Reads on Emotional Intelligence*. Boston: Harvard Business Review Press, 2015.

Hirsch, Sherre. *Thresholds: How to Thrive through Life's Transitions to Live Fearlessly and Regret-Free*. New York: Harmony Books, 2015.

Kabat-Zinn, Jon. *The Mind's Own Physician: A Scientific Dialogue with the Dalai Lama on the Healing Power of Meditation*. Oakland, CA: New Harbinger Publications, 2013.

_____. *Wherever You Go, There You Are: Mindfulness Meditation in Everyday Life*. New York: Hyperion, 1994.

Kabat-Zinn, Myla, and Jon Kabat-Zinn. *Everyday Blessings: The Inner Work of Mindful Parenting*. New York: Hachette Books, 2014.

Katie, Byron, and Stephen Mitchell. *Loving What Is: Four Questions That Can Change Your Life*. New York: Harmony Books, 2002.

Kinder, George. *The Seven Stages of Money Maturity: Cultivating Ease and Freedom in Your Relationship to Money*. New York: Delacorte Press, 1999.

Levine, Amir, and Rachel Heller. *Attached: The New Science of Adult Attachment and How It Can Help You Find—and Keep—Love*. New York: Jeremy P. Tarcher, 2014.

Morinis, Alan. *Everyday Holiness: The Jewish Spiritual Path of Mussar*. Boston: Trumpeter Books, 2009.

Murphy, James D. *Flawless Execution: Use the Techniques and Systems of America's Fighter Pilots to Perform at Your Peak and Win the Battles of the Business World*. New York: Regan Books, 2005.

Neff, Kristin. *Self-Compassion: The Proven Power of Being Kind to Yourself*. London: Hodder & Stoughton, 2013.

Northwestern University Student Affairs. "Wellness at Northwestern: Eight Dimensions of Wellness Overview." northwestern.edu/wellness/8-dimensions.

Paulus, Trina, and Rob Simpson. *Hope for the Flowers*. Old Greenwich, CT: Listening Library and Paulist Press, 1997.

Prochaska, James O., John C. Norcross, and Carlo C. DiClemente. *Changing for Good: A Revolutionary Six-Stage Program for Overcoming Bad Habits and Moving Your Life Positively Forward*. New York: HarpersCollins, 1995.

Rath, Tom. *Strengthsfinder 2.0*. Washington, DC: Gallup Press, 2013.

Rezac, Matthew. *Mindfulness Activities for Adults: 50 Simple Exercises to Relax, Stay Present, and Find Peace*. Emeryville, CA: Rockridge Press, 2021.

Rilke, Rainer Maria. *Letters to a Young Poet: The Possibility of Being*. Translated by Joan M. Burnham. Novato, CA: New World Library, 2000.

Rosenberg, Marshall B. *Nonviolent Communication: A Language of Compassion*. Del Mar, CA: PuddleDancer Press, 2002.

Salzberg, Sharon. *Lovingkindness: The Revolutionary Art of Happiness*. Boston: Shambhala, 2004.

Schwartz, Richard C. *No Bad Parts: Healing Trauma and Restoring Wholeness with the Internal Family Systems Model*. Boulder, CO: Sounds True, 2021.

_____. *You Are the One You've Been Waiting For: Bringing Courageous Love to Intimate Relationships*. Oak Park, IL: Trailheads, 2008.

Sharma, Robin. "4 Reasons to Set Goals." robinsharma.com/article/4-reasons-to -set-goals.

Stone, Douglas, Bruce Patton, and Sheila Heen. *Difficult Conversations: How to Discuss What Matters Most*. London: Penguin Books, 2020.

Wallace, Mary Ann, and Susannah Doyle. *Mindful Eating, Mindful Life: How to Change the Habits That Sabotage Your Health*. Portland, OR: Inkwater, 2010.

Whitfield, Charles L., and Cardwell C. Nuckols. *Healing the Child Within: Discovery and Recovery for Adult Children of Dysfunctional Families*. Deerfield Beach, FL: Health Communications, 2015.

INDEX

conflict, 6, 16–17, 19
connection, 5, 17, 25, 29, 115, 118
Cooper, Stewart E., 4
core Self, 120
  survey, 11
courage, 5, 42, 65, 75, 102, 115
COVID-19, 115
creativity, 5, 33, 115
curiosity, 5, 33, 74, 115

D

denial, 64, 82, 89, 94
depression, 3
diabetes, 47
Dickens, Charles, 2
divorce, 6, 9, 71, 107
Dweck, Carol, 8

E

ego, 3
Empire Strikes Back, 21
exiles, 5

F

failure
  embracing, 21, 97, 103, 111
  fear of, 29, 47, 105, 114
fear
  as inertia (energizing), 48–49
  moving through, 47, 68
feelings
  of anxiety, 3, 23, 28–29
  of failure, 29, 47, 105, 114
  of fear, 48–49, 68

irritability, 80–81
mapping out, 69
of purpose, 53, 80, 106
vulnerable, 105, 112
fixed mindset, 8–10, 105, 116
Freud, Sigmund, 3

G

genetics, 1, 4
goals
  defining, 44
  setting with purpose, 19, 45, 48, 59,
    94 *See also* SMART goals
grief, 23
growth
  mindset, 8–10, 12, 105
  personal, 16–17, 23, 30, 35, 42, 99, 113
  process, 18, 29, 47, 50, 74, 105, 116
grumpiness, 23

H

Harry Potter, 7
horizon contract, 90
hormones, 22
Horney, Karen, 3
hurt feelings, 9, 16, 59, 89

I

imperfections, 12, 115, 127
Internal Family Systems (IFS)
  coaching, 77, 115
  energy, experiencing, 29–30
  experiences of self, 4–5, 17

ACKNOWLEDGMENTS

Deep gratitude to my husband, Matt, for his relentless support while I typed away on this manuscript and expanded my life coaching business—all during the first two months of our marriage. I promise you, it gets better!

Thank you to the countless teachers, patients, clients, students, and supervisees who had to deal with me while I was still in the process of writing my new story of me. I am better for having known you.

My teachers and colleagues at the Mindfulness Coaching School are woven through every page. Matt Rezac, I owe you every success I've had as a coach so far. Rachel Meginnes, Melissa Knorr, Mindy Dow, Diego Ochoa Maynez, Zsanett Czifrus, and Lee Vance have all provided immeasurable support throughout my first year of business and the writing of this book.

ABOUT THE AUTHOR

Yael Dennis, MD, PhD, is a mindfulness-based life coach. She offers Mindful Dating Coaching to people who are single but don't want to be. She also helps people who feel like something is missing in their lives find the sweet spot where passion, purpose, and paycheck meet. She is a former psychiatrist with a decade of clinical experience. She has a doctorate in theology and has spent more than a decade in higher education and training in mindfulness coaching. She lives and works (via Zoom) in Tucson, Arizona. You can find her at BechiraCoaching.com.